UTILIZING EVALUATION

Volume 6
SAGE RESEARCH PROGRESS SERIES IN EVALUATION

SAGE RESEARCH PROGRESS SERIES IN EVALUATION

General Editor: SUSAN E. SALASIN, *National Institute of Mental Health*
Co-Editor (1980): LOIS-ELLIN DATTA, *National Institute of Education*

EDITORIAL REVIEW BOARD

The Series Editors and the Publishers are grateful to those Board members who refereed this year's volumes.

SAGE RESEARCH PROGRESS SERIES IN EVALUATION
Volume 6

Edited by
JAMES A. CIARLO

UTILIZING EVALUATION
Concepts and Measurement Techniques

Published in cooperation with the
EVALUATION RESEARCH SOCIETY

 SAGE PUBLICATIONS   Beverly Hills   London

For information address:

SAGE Publications, Inc.
275 South Beverly Drive
Beverly Hills, California 90212

SAGE Publications Ltd
28 Banner Street
London EC1Y 8QE, England

Printed in the United States of America

Library of Congress Cataloging in Publication Data
Main entry under title:

Utilizing evaluation.

(Sage research progress series in evaluation; v. 6)
"Published in cooperation with the Evaluation Research Society."
Bibliography: p.
1. Evaluation research (Social action programs)—United States—Utilization—Addresses, essays, lectures. I. Ciarlo, James A. II. Series.
H62.U75   361.6'1'0724   80-25821
ISBN 0-8039-1521-7
ISBN 0-8039-1522-5 (pbk.)

FIRST PRINTING

CONTENTS

ABOUT THIS SERIES

The SAGE RESEARCH PROGRESS SERIES IN EVALUATION is a series of concisely edited works designed to present notable, previously unpublished writing on topics of current concern to the evaluation community. In keeping with a vision of evaluation as a methodological enterprise with outcomes at both the policy-making and services delivery levels, the series is designed to present state-of-the-art volumes for use by instructors and students of evaluation, researchers, practitioners, policy-makers, and program administrators.

Each volume (4 to 6 new titles will be published in each calendar year) focuses on themes which emerge from the previous year's annual meeting of the Evaluation Research Society—revised and supplemented by specially commissioned works.

The volumes for 1980 stem primarily from papers delivered at the 3rd Annual Meeting of the Evaluation Research Society held in Minneapolis, Minnesota on October 17-20, 1979. These volumes are:

UTILIZING EVALUATION: Concepts and Measurement Techniques, edited by James A. Ciarlo

EVALUATING VICTIM SERVICES, edited by Susan Salasin

EDUCATING POLICYMAKERS FOR EVALUATION, edited by Keith E. Marvin and Franklin M. Zweig

METHODS FOR EVALUATING HEALTH SERVICES, edited by Paul M. Wortman

Other volumes available in this series are:

*QUALITATIVE AND QUANTITATIVE METHODS IN EVALUA-
TION RESEARCH*, edited by Thomas D. Cook and Charles S.
Reichardt

EVALUATOR INTERVENTIONS: Pros and Cons, edited by Robert
Perloff

TRANSLATING EVALUATION INTO POLICY, edited by Robert F.
Rich

THE EVALUATOR AND MANAGEMENT, edited by Herbert C.
Schulberg and Jeanette M. Jerrell

EVALUATION IN LEGISLATION, edited by Franklin M. Zweig

We are pleased that these volumes in the *SAGE RESEARCH PROG-
RESS SERIES IN EVALUATION* so well represent significant inter-
disciplinary contributions to the literature. Comments and suggestions
from our readers will be welcomed.

SERIES EDITORS:

Susan E. Salasin, National Institute of Mental Health
Lois-ellin Datta, National Institute of Education

EDITOR'S INTRODUCTION

This book is mostly about assessment or measurement, an often abstruse topic that traces all the way back to its basic roots in the philosophy of science. We will not, however, take the reader very far into this rather abstract but well-developed discipline; in fact, we will hardly enter it. Instead, our authors will spend most of their time discussing basic assessment issues or very simple measures of an interesting phenomenon— the utilization of certain kinds of information by persons involved in a variety of human enterprises we call "programs" (health and mental health service programs, welfare programs, educational programs, and the like). We are particularly interested in utilization of the kind of information known as *evaluation*, although one of our authors discusses utilization of program-relevant *research* and another the utilization of *consultants' suggestions* for program improvement. But the common theme is whether program people absorb such program-related information, and how, when, and what, if anything, they then do with respect to the programs they operate.

THE IMPORTANCE OF UTILIZATION STUDIES

Why should we be interested in these phenomena and in research studies that involve measuring utilization?

One answer is that our society increasingly seems to be looking to formal research and evaluations for help in keeping these large-scale programs "accountable," in the sense of demonstrating that they are indeed on track and performing in accordance with goals or expectations. A fair next question, then, is "Do those who call for and fund evaluation studies actually use them in this way?" Despite our often strong impressions about the impacts of evaluation feedback (especially among those of us who labor long and hard over such reports), the only way to answer it with confidence is to do a study of people's actual responses to the evaluation—that is, a utilization study.

A closely related societal function is the identification and selection of the best (or at least better) programs to address and ameliorate particular social problems, such as poverty, sickle-cell anemia, or school drop-out. Again, evaluations and research are increasingly expected to provide guidance in the choice of some programs over others. What utilization studies are available, however, do not clearly indicate that this is happening with sufficient frequency and regularity to resolve all our concerns about making good use of the sizable social investment in research and evaluation activities. While we often hear that profit-making corporations, subjected to the relentless pressures of the competitive market place, are therefore quite sensitive to the latest product developments coming from their "R and D" divisions, we hear no similar refrains about the responsiveness of bureaucrats and legislators to the latest information regarding innovations in school, welfare, or mental health programs. Is this true, and, if so, why? Again, we must turn to those who study the utilization of information for some answers.

THE IMPACT OF UTILIZATION ON EVALUATION

Evaluation appears to be increasingly linked to *change* in the ways society chooses to do things. It follows that society as a whole, as well as evaluators and researchers engaged in change efforts, may have a good deal to lose if utilization of such information is slow, erratic, and infrequent.

First, society's expectations of assistance from evaluators can be largely unrealized, with consequent criticism of evaluation as "impotent" that is actually unjustified. In addition, cynicism regarding evaluation may develop, so that it is perceived as wasteful, or nothing more then "eyewash," or at best useful only as a political or public relations tool. The real contribution of the evaluation field to society, in terms of knowledge of program results, could thus be minimized.

Second, evaluators personally may experience discouragement at lack of utilization that causes them to cut short their potentially valuable careers of service to society. Many of us already know a few idealistic, but disillusioned, people who have left evaluation when less frustrating opportunities came along. Again, society (and perhaps the individual) is likely to have lost something.

We can hopefully avoid these negative consequences of under- or nonutilization of evaluation and research by learning more about utilization and applying that knowledge directly to the evaluation enterprise. Specifically:

(1) We can try to determine accurately the true magnitude or degree of utilization of evaluation in a variety of circumstances, its timing and locus, and the eventual consequences of the utilization in terms of program improvement.

(2) We can improve our theoretical understanding of utilization through empirical studies, especially studies of what factors mediate effective utilization or nonutilization.

(3) We may even be able to develop "tools" for increasing the impact of evaluation. The Davis "checklist"[1] of decision determinants to be considered by purveyors of program-related information is an early example of such a tool.

SOME UNRESOLVED ISSUES IN STUDYING UTILIZATION

It is easy to set forth a number of good reasons to study utilization. It is far more difficult to say just *how* such studies should be done, and particularly how utilization should be assessed or measured. This collection of articles represents the thinking and experience of a group of people who have been involved in utilization measurement efforts. As the reader will soon note, disagreements on a number of key issues are apparent.

What Should We Measure?

Perhaps the first and foremost issues is the conceptualization of just what we should be looking for when we develop measures of utilization. Our lead author, Carol Weiss, argues here, as she has elsewhere, that it is a mistake to set as a criterion of utilization the direct adoption of evaluation-based recommendations by an agency or program. Instead, she argues for a very broad, somewhat diffuse concept of utilization that would include such things as changing people's orientation slightly, justification of already existing actions, stimulating further inquiry, and "tucking suggestions away for future consideration." In this view she adopts a position somewhat like Patton's, who has argued for a subjective "reduction in uncertainty" as a sufficient and appropriate criterion for indicating utilization. In contrast, most of our other authors, such as Larsen and Anderson et al., place much more weight on actual changes in the programs as evidencing utilization. Stevenson, after criticizing the uncertainty-reduction criterion, also calls for clear, objective evidence for utilization of at least some types of evaluation, including evaluations directed at procedural recommendations and those involving a demonstration project.

Several of these chapters, however, also discuss utilization criteria other than adoption of recommendations or program change. The field has moved beyond the simple "adoption" criterion of use (*instrumental* utilization) and now allows for changes in thinking without accompanying overt action as evidence of utilization (*conceptual* utilization). This differentiation, however, raises additional problems with the studies done to date. Most investigators either do *not* study both types of utilization or do not clearly differentiate between the factors that are expected to lead to one or the other; it is assumed that the study results hold for both kinds of, or undifferentiated, utilization. Furthermore, the procedures used to measure utilization are usually not tailored carefully to the type of utilization the investigator is looking for—and this brings up the second major unresolved issue we wish to note here.

The Quality and Precision of Utilization Measurement

As Conner notes in his chapter, the derivation of conclusions about how much utilization has occurred, and what factors facilitated or impeded utilization, has so far rested almost solely upon loosely structured interviews or questionnaires with key possible users of an evaluation or research study. In these studies, the investigators draw conclusions from certain portions of these interviews, and then buttress them by citing key respondent sentences which illustrate the points being made. However, they also use coding systems, apparently to organize the responses into more precise categories. Sometimes these category frequencies are referred to in the articles, but the analysis of utilization to date remains remarkably nonquantitative and dependent on unstandardized verbal reports. Unfortunately, the authors usually do not publish the coding system they used (at least in sufficient detail to allow another user to replicate their study), and there seems to be no common coding scheme in use among the leaders in this area.

To be sure, this may be a product of the viewpoint articulated by Weiss and others that utilization criteria *should* remain global and broad at this point. Yet it is probably true that when we remain highly global and sensitive to nuances, we also may see in a response just what we expect to see, and what others may *not* see. As Conner notes, there are no published coding reliability figures for the key studies he reviews, and the same is true for most other studies this writer has read. We may have reason, then, to question the solidity of even the few pieces of knowledge about utilization that we think we have.

In contrast to most writings on utilization, the Larsen and Anderson et al. chapters in this volume deal quite specifically with the issue of quantifying measures of utilization, and Anderson goes into some detail regarding the reliability of the coding procedure for "behavioral" (instrumental) utilization. Stevenson also provides advice regarding selection of quantitative indices that would be appropriate to evidence utilization, and Pelz and Horsley discuss their use of standardized questionnaires with quantitative responses in their efforts to demonstrate the effects of special training of nurses in the utilization of practice-relevant research.

Finally, investigators in the utilization field *must* begin to deal with the issue of obtaining "socially desirable" responses regarding the utilization of research and evaluation. It is to be expected that most persons will want to say, when interviewed, that they *did* read an evaluation report, they *did* think about it, and it had *some* effect on their thinking about their program even if they took no direct or specific action on it. But how much of this is really true? What modern program manager is going to forthrightly state that he is *not* giving any weight to evaluation feedback in his subsequent decision making? To do so might reflect directly upon his managerial capacity—or at least he may think so. And if we find some relationships of other variables with such self-reported "utilization" measures, could it not be relationships with *truthfulness* or *social independence* that we have actually found? Until we begin to find ways of buttressing verbal reports of utilization with supplemental evidence such as decision memos, shifts in program operating statistics, or at least concurrence among several people that an evaluation finding was indeed discussed, or considered, or seemed to influence a subsequent decision, the relationships we find may be evanescent—found here, today, but nowhere to be seen elsewhere or tomorrow.

There are many other issues discussed, or at least reflected, in this series of articles. Weiss offers a taxonomy of methods to study different aspects of utilization and lists their strengths and weaknesses. Conner raises the issue of what organizational levels should be included among respondents being asked about utilization. Anderson et al. suggest the addition of *affective* utilization, or a change in emotional state or feeling about programs, to other types already identified by investigators. There are numerous others that will be readily apparent to readers, some important, others offering just a finer distinction regarding some aspect of utilization rather than a major assessment or measurement issue. With the hope that the reader will find useful suggestions for conceptualizing the assessment of utilization, and for managing to measure it with greater reliability and validity than it typically has been, I refer the reader to the chapters that follow.

James A. Ciarlo

NOTE

1. Readers may find this checklist, as well as other suggestions for increasing utilization, in National Institute of Mental Health (1971: 27-30), Planning for creative change in mental health services: A manual on research utilization. DHEW Publication No. (HSM) 71-9059. Washington, DC: Government Printing Office.

In the lead chapter, Weiss sets forth her arguments for holding to a broad view of utilization, one that accepts a significantly wider range of evidence for use of evaluation than just direct action on findings or recommendations. She then sets out four approaches to the study of utilization that link directly to methods that would best be employed. Using this schema, she is able to point out the strengths and weaknesses of the various assessment methods that have been used—and perhaps not surprisingly, it turns out that what is good in one situation may be a poor choice of method in another.

Although the chapter by Stevenson uses a local agency as the setting for a discussion of utilization and its assessment, the article ranges more widely and includes a perceptive analysis and critique of the highly subjective "reduction of uncertainty" criterion for evaluation utilization. He then moves into his own schema for relating appropriate criteria for assessment of utilization to the original purpose of the evaluation. He also deals sensitively with the dilemma of an evaluator trying to fairly and objectively assess a program upon which he is dependent for not only his job but also his own success as a professional evaluator.

The chapter by Conner consists of a comparative analysis and overall critique of eight key utilization studies in several areas. Most of the studies did not involve utilization of evaluation feedback, but rather the impact of a wide range of social research studies upon local and federal government policy formation. Nevertheless, the similarity to the problem of evaluation utilization is great, as is made clear in Conners' multidimensional analysis of the actual measurement processes. He concludes that our assessment methods should be improved in a number of ways, including the assurance of reliability of the scores derived from the various types of measures employed.

Larsen and Werner take up the basic problem of deriving a quantitative measurement of utilization from essentially qualitative, "categorical" data that seem to denote alternative outcomes of program consultation by experts to a number of different community mental health centers. Again, the basic similarity to the problem of evaluation utilization is high, although more complexity is introduced in the form of an "outsider" with personal and professional characteristics that, along with the basic quality and soundness of the ideas presented, could influence use of his or her suggestions. These authors also begin to deal with an aspect of any idea, research finding, or evaluation recommendation that could be presented for possible utilization—the expected difficulty of implementing that recommendation or suggestion.

The chapter by Anderson and her coauthors is essentially a detailed description of how evaluation utilization was conceptualized and measured after evaluation feedback to a series of local mental health service units. The authors not only present their efforts to assess what actually happens to the units' services as a result of evaluative feedback but they also show how they try to systematically capture changes in staff thinking that may not surface into actual behavior, at least within the time of postfeedback follow-up. Another contribution is the suggestion that personal utilization of feedback may also be reflected in the emotional sector; for example, program staff may report feeling much better (or worse) about their service efforts depending on what the evaluation feedback shows about how they are performing on a difficult task.

The article by Pelz and Horsley deals with the measurement of research utilization in the context of an intensive effort to train nurses to bring new research-based ideas into their care activities. The focus is both on assessment of utilization activities directly related to the training (reviewing research literature, planning implementation of new practices) and on more indirect evidence of changes in the nurses' daily care practices that could result from training. A good feature of some of the utilization measures is their quantification in terms of frequency of specific activities, thus anchoring the scales to presumably objective and potentially quite reliable evidence of utilization.

1

MEASURING THE USE OF EVALUATION

Carol H. Weiss

Harvard University

Studying the effects of social science research and evaluation used to be a problematic enterprise, and anyone writing on the subject had to justify its importance. Nowadays people in many places are concerned about the effects of research and evaluation on the development and improvement of social programs. It has become a matter of some moment to know *how much* contribution systematic research makes to effective programming and *how, when,* and *where* it has its major influence.[1] We can take the significance of the questions for granted. The challenge is to get on with the job.

This article addresses two issues that must be considered in getting on with the job of studying uses. The first is the definition of what we mean by research use, so that we can recognize it when we see it. The second is the design of how we study it, the entry point for inquiry and the tracers that supply evidence.

RESEARCH UTILIZATION: WHAT IS IT?

Research utilization sounds like a straightforward and obvious event. Particularly in a local agency, there seems little complexity in seeing whether a study has been used. Once a study has been done—say, an evaluation of one particular strategy of service—it should be clear whether the agency managers and program practitioners have adopted the strategy that was found successful, abandoned the strategy found unsuccessful, or modified existing strategy in accordance with the conclusions and recommendations of the study. To study use, one would think, you look at program managers' decisions about the program and see whether they have followed the import of the data and/or the explicit recommendations of the evaluator. That used to be the traditional formulation, and in some places it still is.

This article takes issue with that formulation of "research utilization." I suggest that it embodies an inappropriate imagery, and in fact goes so far as to abandon the term *utilization* because of its overtones of instrumental episodic application. People do not utilize research the way that they utilize a hammer. The whole process through which research penetrates the sphere of organizational decision making—the processes of understanding, accepting, reorienting, adapting, and applying research results to the world of practice—is more fluid and diffuse than the earlier image implied.

Let me give five examples of the interaction between the conclusions of an evaluation study and the acts of agency managers. Each of them illustrates that the traditional notion of research utilization, as supplying "answers" that program managers "adopt" to "solve" a problem, may be an inappropriate way to think about the subject.

ILLUSTRATIONS OF EVALUATION-PROGRAM INTERACTIONS

First, take the case of an evaluation study that does not produce forthright answers. It finds modest successes in some areas of program operation and modest shortcomings in other areas, without giving clear-cut direction for expansion, modification, or termination of the program. Many studies produce this kind of inconclusive evidence. There is "on the one hand," but there is also "on the other hand." What one does with findings of this sort is indeterminate.

Some evaluation studies discover an absence of expected effects, but cannot attribute the failure to any particular activities of the program or its staff. They do not reveal whether the basic theory of the program is wrong (i.e., that its activities are inherently unable to alter the behaviors that it aims to change) or whether the failings are due to the special conditions and disadvantages of the immediate setting. Therefore, the evaluation cannot say with any confidence whether the remedy is to abandon the program or to try to operate it more effectively.

In sum, evaluations do not always—or even often—come up with data that give explicit guidance for action. Therefore, it becomes difficult to study the "use" made of the study by monitoring the agency's adoption of the "answer" that the study supplied.

Because many evaluation studies—particularly those conducted in a single agency—do not have sufficient comparative data to specify the factors that contributed to program success or program failure, the evaluator makes a leap from the data in developing recommendations. She uses judgment—as well as science—in drawing implications for action. In the not infrequent case when outcomes are mixed (some indicators go up while others do not, or some clients benefit but others fail to benefit), the data may not lead to any direct lessons. The evaluator, in making recommendations, is inevitably guided by her own standards, beliefs, and predilections, her sense of what is possible and feasible, what costs too much or will encounter resistance, her knowledge of alternative possibilities and their likelihood of success. To study the "use" of evaluation by looking at the agency's adoption of the *recommendations* is in effect to study the use of the evaluator's judgment. It is not obvious that this is a study of the use of evaluation.

Consider a second case where one evaluation study comes up with one set of findings, while another evaluation of the same or a very similar program comes up with discrepant findings. Members of the program staff divide into two camps, one group advocating the implementation of the recommendations derived from the first study and a second group pushing for acceptance of the recommendations based on the second study. In such a situation, there will undoubtedly be people who insist on doing nothing until better information becomes available and the discrepancies are resolved. They are likely to prevail—at least for a time, while the agency searches for further data.

How does one assess the use of evaluation under these circumstances? No one can assert that the evaluations are not getting a hearing, but nothing seems to be happening in the program. No action is being taken that appears responsive to either evaluation. The person who is studying the use of evaluations by looking at program decisions is likely to conclude that the studies were not used. Perhaps two or three years later, after further evidence has accumulated from new evaluations or other sources, some of the findings from the earlier studies will be reinforced and gain in credibility, and significant changes will be introduced. But by that time, the student of the uses of evaluation will probably have come and gone.

These two examples indicate the frequent fragility of the "answer" that evaluation supplies. It is often incomplete, merged with nonresearch judgment, incompatible with or contradicted by other evaluation evidence, and only a partial guide to responsible action. This is not to say, of course, that it is valueless. The information from evaluation may well be the best information on program outcome around, and it usually has important implications for program managers. The significant point is that to study its use *only* in terms of immediate and direct impact on program decisions is unduly constricting.

Let us take a third case in which an agency encounters neither particular problems nor clearly defined decision points. The program has been operating and continues to operate. No decisions are pending about funding, staffing, clientele, or activities, or about expansion or contraction of the program. An evaluation is done that points out areas of potential improvement. People read the report and take it seriously, but there seems little opportunity to put the findings to work in obvious ways. They have a limited budget, staff with particular skills, a building not located in an optimal site but serviceable—and things are going pretty well. They have neither the motivation nor the opportunity to apply the evaluation findings; no decision has to be made and they make none. They tuck the suggestions away for future consideration when conditions change. But again, there is no visible effect on decisions.

The fourth illustration concerns an agency that confronts neither inconclusive evaluation results nor absence of decisional choices. Decisions about the future have to be made, and the evaluation study provides direction and recommendations for change. But the evidence that the study offers about program outcomes is only one kind of information that managers take into account. They also consider the costs of program modifications, the types of staff needed to implement the modifications, the wishes of client groups, the preferences of referring agencies, and the program emphases of federal sponsors. Let us suppose that some or all of these factors militate against the actions suggested by the evaluation. After weighing all the evidence, managers conclude that the other factors are more important and decide not to follow the prescriptions derived from evaluation. Anyone going in to study the use of evaluation according to the simple rule ("See if the decision followed the advice based on evaluation") would conclude that the study was not used. In fact, it stimulated significant review of the program. Even though its conclusions were

outweighed by competing concerns of cost, staff capabilities, client demands, interagency relationships, or political feasibility, it illuminated
problems, clarified trade-offs, and evoked new understandings of the
possibilities and limits of program action.

Let us consider a final case. Program managers have developed plans to
make changes in their program for reasons that have little to do with
program effectiveness and much to do with the survival of their agency.
An evaluation is done and points out shortcomings in the program. The
managers take advantage of the opportunity to institute the changes that
they have already planned. The action they take is not exactly what the
evaluation report recommends, but it appears to be directed at problems
that the evaluation has uncovered and responsive to evaluation conclusions. Is this a use of evaluation? The person looking at the outcome by
the rule of thumb, "See if the decision followed the evaluation-based
advice," might be misled. He would assume that the evaluation was used as
a basis of decision, although in this case the change was contemplated long
before the evaluation—and on other grounds. But in a different sense, the
evaluation *was* "used": It provided an opportunity to bring about changes
that the program staff wanted and it helped to legitimate their actions. Is
that a legitimate use?

These kinds of cases are legion. They make the study of the effects of
evaluation research a difficult enterprise. When the action that evaluation
implies is unclear, or when different studies point in different directions,
when organizational and political conditions leave little opportunity for
implementing evaluation results, when competing constraints swamp evaluation evidence, when changes occur only after protracted periods of time,
when staff use evaluation to legitimate changes they had already decided
upon—how does the student of use of evaluation make sense of what is
going on? To limit our attention to direct and immediate application of
evaluation results to decisions forecloses the opportunity to understand
how evaluations in fact affect program operation. We see only the small
slice of the action that falls within our arbitrary definition of use and fail
to examine the scores of subtle effects that may turn out to have
cumulative consequences of major dimensions.

What makes the conventional approach to the study of use even more
troublesome is the implicit assumption that use is good and nonuse is bad.
Use of evaluation results seems to signify the triumph of science, reason,
objective evidence, and dispassionate social scientists over the forces of
inertia, agency politics, stupidity, and the self-servingness of managers and
professionals. The notion that evaluations may be tinged with their own

biases and that they do not always supply the final word gets little consideration—nor does the possibility that program managers and staffs have knowledge and judgment derived from sources other than evaluation. It is a myopic—and astigmatic—view of the agency world.

What often happens when agencies confront evaluations is even more complex than the five vignettes imply. In many cases, what evaluation research provides to program agencies is not so much specific evidence about the success or failure of particular programs as rich information about the contexts in which programs operate. Evaluation research can serve highly useful purposes by illuminating the backdrop against which choices must be made. It can provide information about clients (their problems, expectations, lifestyles, and motives), about programs (standards of selection of recipients, daily activities, resources, limits, modes of coping with obstacles, theories-in-use), about staff, and about the agency environment. Richly textured information of this kind can fill in pieces of what Patton et al. (1977) have called the puzzle of agency action.

Another major contribution that evaluation research often makes is to build up generalizations about program theory. It generates ideas about the kinds of interventions that work in given circumstances and the kinds of interventions that fail. It says something about which theories of programming are empirically supported and the conditions under which they hold. One study of one program (even of a program as administered at multiple sites) can be discounted on the basis of weaknesses in methodology. There is almost always some flaw that critics can find to justify disregarding the study's results—and often rightly so: The sample was too small, the time period too short, the study begun too soon after the program's start, the control groups corrupted, the measures too soft or too narrow or too remote from the program's central goals, the analysis inappropriate, or the recommendations too global or insufficiently supported by the evidence presented. One study, particularly a study that has had to make methodological compromises, is often fragile support for major programmatic revision.

But a body of evaluation studies, conducted by different investigators using different methodologies, often converge on a theme. And it is this theme, this orienting perspective, this generalization about programming that comes into currency. Some examples of ideas that have come from waves of evaluation studies would be: Released mental patients do not fare well in the community unless given intensive personal support services, in-school compensatory education programs for junior high and high school students do not overcome educational deficiencies, poor people use health services as extensively as other people when the services are available and convenient. And program managers and other decision makers use these kinds of ideas in making decisions about programs—even when the studies were not conducted on their own programs and *even when they cannot cite the studies from which the generalizations come.* They have absorbed the generalizations from diverse sources over a period of time, and these ideas become the taken-for-granted assumptions on which they base new plans and decisions. Social scientists studying the uses of evaluation research studies by traditional methods are very likely to overlook this kind of use entirely.

Students of research use have made a distinction between "instrumental use," in which research or evaluation conclusions are applied to a specific decision, and "conceptual use," in which research affects the understanding of issues more broadly (Caplan et al., 1975; Rich and Caplan, 1976; Weiss, 1977; Rich, 1977; Pelz, 1978). This is a useful distinction because it indicates that the use of research can take different forms. It recognizes that research can have consequences not only when people adopt its conclusions directly but also when they are influenced by its concepts and ideas.

As Caplan (1977), Caplan et al. (1975), Rich (1977), Patton et al. (1977), and others have shown empirically, conceptual use is likely to be more prevalent than instrumental use. It may also be more significant. Instrumental use is often restricted to relatively low-level decisions, where the stakes are small and users' interests relatively unaffected. Conceptual use, which does not involve immediate and direct application of conclusions to decisions, can gradually bring about major shifts in awareness and reorientation of basic perspectives.

While the categories of instrumental and conceptual use have served a useful purpose (they have helped in making the transition from our original exclusive preoccupation with instrumental use), I now believe that they are somewhat arbitrary. The use of research and evaluation is actually a continuum. At one end are those few cases where research actually switches a decision from A to B by the power of its evidence and analysis. In the middle are the many cases where research evidence is taken into account but does not drive the decision—cases where users filter research evidence through their knowledge, judgment, and interests, and incorporate much besides research into decision making. At the far end are the large array of issues on which research contributes more diffusely to an understanding of issues, the causes of problems, and the dynamics of intervention. For people who are concerned with the effects of research and evaluation on social programming, most of the phenomena of interest probably lie in the large and unbounded middle ground.

CONCEPTUALIZATION OF USE

Clearly a central issue for the study of the uses of evaluation, research, and analysis is: What constitutes a use? The direct implementation of specific evaluation conclusions in immediate decisions about the future of the program studied is only one kind of use—and it appears to be relatively infrequent. But there are many other kinds of uses where evaluation conclusions affect ideas about programming indirectly, over time, as part of a larger body of information, with less obvious consequences. To leave them out of our purview would represent a serious underestimate of the effects of research.

To clarify the concept of "use," we have to confront prickly questions. We have to specify such dimensions as these:

(1) *What is used.* Do we define the "what" as recommendations from one study, data and conclusions from one study, some *part* of the data, findings from a series of related studies, generalizations derived from a synthesis of studies, social science concepts used in the studies? Do we include findings that have been selectively plucked from research, or misunderstood, or distorted?

(2) *How direct is the derivation from the study.* Does "use" require that people read the original report, a summary written by the authors of the report, a description by someone else *about* the report? How about a conversation with the evaluator, a second-hand account from somebody who talked to the evaluator, or a staff person's recollection that there was "an evaluation on this"?

(3) *By whom it is used.* Decisions in organizations are rarely the province of one individual. Decisions require agreement and sign-offs at multiple levels. Do we limit certified users to the immediate program decision makers, include other staff in the agency, officials at other levels (federal, state, local)? How about direct-service staff who may modify some of their day-to-day behavior, or interest groups who may lobby for program change, or clients who learn from evaluation about the likelihood of program success and give or withdraw their support and attendance?

(4) *By how many people it is used.* Is it enough if one aide to a decision maker reads the report and forcefully propounds its lessons to her boss? Or is there some minimal penetration of the decision-making group that must be achieved?

(5) *How immediate is the use.* Does use have to take place shortly after the study was done? Is it a use if study conclusions are considered and

weighed over the longer term? What about the gradual percolation of evaluation results and ideas into agency deliberations?

(6) Most important of all, *how much effect is required.* To count as a "use" must every one of the evaluation recommendations be adopted? What if some recommendations are adopted but not others? Or suppose the evaluation stimulates review and rethinking but different changes from those recommended are adopted. What if evaluation results are given a thoughtful hearing but are purposely set aside under the weight of other factors? Or suppose the ideas from evaluation and research help people make sense of what they are doing and give them a new perspective on the program. Suppose they conclude that their current goals are excessively optimistic and unrealistic and scale down their goals. Or they begin long-range exploration of alternative agency missions. Or they find new grounds to justify what they are already doing. Are these "uses"? If evaluation results are given a hearing and affect opinions and ideas about programming, even in unintended ways, how do we rule some "in" and some "out" of the definition of use?

These are some of the conceptual issues that people who study the use of research and evaluation must grapple with. They are troublesome questions, particularly because some uses look "good" and others look "bad." To adopt evaluation recommendations looks "good," at least to evaluators. To cite evaluation as support for changes that would have been made anyway looks "bad," although it may be a highly effective merger of managerial experience and evaluation evidence. *Until we resolve questions about the definition of use, we face a future of noncomparable studies of use and scant hope of cumulative understanding of how evaluation and decision making intersect.*

In my view, the field should adopt a broad construction of the meaning of use at this time. (See also Cohen and Weiss, 1977; Pelz, 1978; Alkin et al., 1979; Rein and White, 1977; Patton et al., 1977; Knorr, 1977; Lindblom and Cohen, 1979.) We should look at the full range of ways in which research and evaluation influence the development of program and policy. To look small, to restrict ourselves to studying immediate applications of findings to decisions, takes for granted a rational theory of organizational behavior. It assumes that organizations make decisions according to a rational model: define problems, generate options, search for information about the relative merits of each option, and then, on the basis of the information, make a choice. As our colleagues who study organizational behavior tell us (Simon, 1976; March and Olsen, 1976; Meyer and Rowan, 1977; Weick, 1969; Mintzberg, 1973; Allison, 1971;

Thompson, 1967; Downs, 1967), this is a patently inaccurate view of how organizations work. When we implicitly adopt this as our underlying theory of organizations in studying research use, we inevitably reach distorted conclusions. Until we can develop better models of how organizations use information, we are best served by examining the spectrum of organizational uses of research and evaluation. We may like some uses and dislike others, but such judgments should not get in the way. We need to *understand* the consequences of research and evaluation for organizational practice. Only with a broad-gauge view will we make headway in this endeavor.

If an excessively rationalistic view of organizational decision making can constrict our understanding of the use of research and evaluation at the agency level, it is almost fatal to understanding at the policy level. Major policy directions taken by federal departments and their component agencies and the Congress are almost never the product of rational analysis alone. They are strongly influenced by legislative politics, bureaucratic politics, constituent interests, competing claims on the federal budget, pressure groups, public acceptance, and a host of idiosyncratic elements. To look only for the incorporation of research and evaluation results in the policies that emerge from the complex play of interests is to ignore almost all of the game. Such a narrow view also ignores the many diffuse ways in which research and evaluation affect, legitimate, and frame the positions that participants take and the bargains that they negotiate. Again, it seems sensible to look broadly at the ways in which research and evaluation help to shape the policy debate.

Once we have agreed on the definition of use, we have to look at the relation between the concept and the craft. How do we go about studying the complex and intricate patterns in which research and evaluation are woven into agency deliberations?

APPROACHES TO THE STUDY OF USE

Investigators who narrowly construe research use generally start with a *study* and try to trace its effects on subsequent decisions. Much has been learned by this strategy of investigation, and it deserves to be pursued further. But there are other approaches to the study of research use as well, some of which have significant potential for expanding our knowledge.

Basically, investigators have adopted four approaches for studying the consequences of research and evaluation. Each of them implies a distinctive type of question and typically uses a different data-collection method. Each of them is well-suited to exploring some issues and less appropriate for investigating others. Here are brief sketches of the four possibilities.

(1) Start with *studies* and follow the effects of the studies on subsequent decisions. This approach has been used to investigate the consequences of a single research study (e.g., Datta, 1976, on the evaluation of Head Start; Boeckmann, 1976, on the New Jersey negative income tax experiment; White, 1975, on evaluation of school performance in Atlanta; Rich, 1975, on the Continuous National Survey; Weiss, 1970, on the federal student loan program), and it has been used to study the effects of multiple studies (e.g., Alkin et al., 1979, studied the uses of five evaluations of Title I and Title IV-C educational programs; Patton et al., 1977, studied the uses of 20 health program evaluations). The basic assumption is that the investigator can ferret out the effects of the study on the people who make significant decisions.

(2) Start with *people* who are prospective users of research and evaluation studies. This is the approach that Caplan et al. (1975) used in their investigation of use. They sent interviewers to talk with federal officials in a wide range of federal departments and asked them about their uses of research—which studies they used, when they used them, how they used them, and the consequences of use (see also Caplan and Barton, 1976). The basic assumption is that people can remember the studies that influenced them and will be candid and accurate in their responses.

(3) Start with an *issue* and examine the ways in which research and evaluation help to shape the resolution of the issue. Aaron (1978) investigated the extent to which research helped to set the agenda, bound the discussion, and influence the direction of federal policy in three areas: poverty and discrimination, education and jobs, and unemployment and inflation. His analysis of the influence of research, evaluation, and policy analysis on the development of policy on these issues is a complex and fascinating study. In a somewhat broader vein, the National Academy of Sciences, panel on Study of the Policy Formation Process is currently studying the gamut of factors that shaped the Women, Infants, and Children nutritional program, the child care tax deduction, and federal interagency day care regulations. Research and evaluation studies are one of the formative factors that are receiving explicit attention. An underlying assumption of studies that focus on an issue, and examine the contribution of research to the progressive decisions on the issue, is that the investigator can separate the studies that actually had an impact on

decision makers from those that did not, and that he can unravel the special contributions that derived from research.

(4) Start with an *organization* and investigate the impact of research and evaluation on the life history of the organization. Studies of this type have to date been done mainly by social scientists concerned with organizational development and have focused on the effects of consultant intervention or the introduction of social-scientific innovations. Some examples[2] are the studies of the effects of social science research and experimentation in hospitals by Jaques's group in Britain (Rowbottom et al., 1973), the study of social scientists' involvement in research and action at the Glacier Metal Company over almost two decades (e.g., Brown and Jaques, 1965), and Klein's (1976) account of the effects of the employment of an in-house social scientist—herself—in the Esso Petroleum Company, Ltd.

These studies examine the changes and the processes of change in organizations that follow upon the introduction of social science research, analysis, and training into large organizations. They do not limit attention to effects on discrete decisions but range more widely over the consequences on structure, plans, priorities, communication, and programs. An assumption is that investigation can track the rippling effects of research on organizational behavior.

Methods of study tend to vary with the approach taken to the study of use. The method is largely determined by the locus of effect that is of primary concern.

Focus of Attention	*Methodological Strategy*
Studies	*Case studies* that trace the impact of the studies on decisions. While organizational records are usually reviewed, particular reliance is placed on interviews with informants.
People	*Surveys.* Interviews are conducted with a sample of potential users of research.
Issues	*Review of documents* (hearings, bills, reports, amendments) that mark the legislative and executive history of the issue. *Review of research studies* relevant to the issue. Documents that bear the

Organizations

impress of research findings (testimony, references) are important for attesting to linkages.

Participant-observation. Since the researchers generally have long-term involvement with the organization, their notes, records, and recollections are primary sources.

The four approaches are directed at somewhat different questions about use. Although each of them can be used to answer a variety of questions, they are shaped by different conceptual and methodological constraints. By virtue of their internal logic, they appear to be best adapted to deal with particular questions.

Focus of Attention	*Questions best answered*	*Questions less well answered*
Studies	How much effect did the study have on decisions at the focal site?	What indirect effects did research have? Did it have effects at other sites? Were there long-term effects?
People	What kinds of people (by position, location, training, etc.) are most likely to use research? How much use do they make of research?	How does one person's use of research interact with others' uses (or non-uses) to influence events? Which available research leaves no impression?
Issues	What is the relative influence of research on the resolution of the issue compared with other information, interests, pressures, and demands?	Through what agents is research use mediated? How does research come to attention? Who promotes consideration of research and for what purposes?
Organizations	How much influence does research have on organizational behavior? Through what channels does research penetrate the organization? What are the consequences?	Why does research have the observed consequences? Are the processes of use unique to this organization?

Finally, let us look at some of the major limitations that attend each methodological strategy. Although some of the limitations can be mitigated by careful design and artful fieldwork, they tend to be the natural spawn of the method. Investigators have to make sedulous efforts to reduce their more serious effects.

Methodological Approach	*Special Limitations Limitations*
Case studies of the effects of research and evaluation	Short span of time under investigation. Informants' lack of knowledge about or sensitivity to the effects of research. Investigator's inability to interview all participants; overattention to the forceful or articulate informant.
Surveys of possible users	Respondents' poor memory of the research that has influenced them, their inability to disentangle research from all the other materials they read; inability to cite references, to recall the conceptual consequences of research, or to trace the steps of research use. Misreporting.
Documentary review of the resolution of issues	Lack of clear evidence of the linkages between research and official acts. Therefore, the investigator may attribute too much influence to a particular study or not enough. Research that influenced some participants may fail to surface.
Participant-observation of organizations	Bias of investigators, who are involved with the organization. Lack of generalizability of one organization's experience: idiosyncratic events, historical circumstances, personalities, time period.

To answer the gamut of unanswered questions about the uses of research and evaluation, none of these approaches is probably sufficient alone. To make progress in our quest for understanding, we need to employ mixed strategies and approach the question from multiple perspectives.

Above all, we need to come to consensus about the meaning of use, so that inquiries about the uses of research and evaluation can study the issue in comparable terms and build a cumulative body of knowledge. Only with clarity about the characterization of use can we proceed to learn (1) which kinds of people (2) in which kinds of contexts (3) make which kinds of uses (4) of which kinds of research and evaluation (5) with what range of consequences.

NOTES

1. The people who are interested in the uses of research and evaluation in policy and practice tend to be policy-oriented researchers and federal officials who fund research and evaluations. Both groups have a self-interested concern in legitimating their work, but they also tend to be professionally committed to the principle of research application for improving the caliber of program decisions. Relatively few policy makers or practitioners have yet paid serious attention to the question of research uses, except for the global, and skeptical, question of whether research and evaluation are ever used—or even usable—at all.

2. I thank Chris Argyris for bringing these studies to my attention.

REFERENCES

AARON, H. J. (1978) Politics and the Professors: The Great Society in Perspective. Washington, DC: Brookings Institution.

ALKIN, M. C., R. DAILLAK, and P. WHITE (1979) Using Evaluations: Does Evaluation Make a Difference? Beverly Hills, CA: Sage.

ALLISON, G. T. (1971) Essence of Decision: Explaining the Cuban Missile Crisis. Boston: Little, Brown.

BOECKMANN, M. E. (1976) "Policy impacts of the New Jersey income maintenance experiment." Policy Sciences 7: 53-76.

BROWN, W. and E. JAQUES (1965) Glacier Project Papers. London: Heinemann.

CAPLAN, N. (1977) "A minimal set of conditions necessary for the utilization of social science knowledge in policy formulation at the national level," pp. 183-197 in C. H. Weiss (ed.) Using Social Research in Public Policy Making. Lexington, MA: Lexington-Heath.

——— and E. BARTON (1976) Social indicators 1973: A study of the relationship between the power of information and utilization by federal executives. Ann Arbor: University of Michigan, Institute for Social Research.

CAPLAN, N., A. MORRISON, and R. J. STAMBAUGH (1975) The use of social science knowledge in policy decisions at the national level: A report to respondents. Ann Arbor: University of Michigan, Center for Research on Utilization of Scientific Knowledge, Institute for Social Research.

COHEN, D. K. and J. A. WEISS (1977) "Social science and social policy: Schools and race," pp. 67-83 in C. H. Weiss (ed.) Using Social Research in Public Policy Making. Lexington, MA: Lexington-Heath.

DATTA, L. (1976) "The impact of the Westinghouse/Ohio evaluation of the development of Project Head Start: An examination of the immediate and longer-term effects and how they came about," pp. 129-181 in C. C. Abt (ed.) The Evaluation of Social Programs. Beverly Hills, CA: Sage.

DOWNS, A. (1967) Inside Bureaucracy. Boston: Little, Brown.

KLEIN, L. (1976) A Social Scientist in Industry. New York: John Wiley.

KNORR, K. D. (1977) "Policymakers' use of social science knowledge: Symbolic or instrumental?" pp. 165-182 in C. H. Weiss (ed.) Using Social Research in Public Policy Making. Lexington, MA: Lexington-Heath.

LINDBLOM, C. E. and D. K. COHEN (1979) Usable Knowledge: Social Science and Social Problem Solving. New Haven, CT: Yale University Press.

MARCH, J. G. and J. P. OLSEN (1976) Ambiguity and Choice in Organizations. Bergen-Oslo-Tromsφ, Norway: Universitetforlaget.

MEYER, J. W. and B. ROWAN (1977) "Institutionalized organizations: Formal structure as myth and ceremony." American Journal of Sociology 83: 340-363.

MINTZBERG, H. (1973) The Nature of Managerial Work. New York: Harper & Row.

PATTON, M. Q., P. S. GRIMES, K. M. GUTHRIE, N. J. BREMAN, B. D. FRENCH, and D. A. BLYTH (1977) "In search of impact: An analysis of the utilization of federal health evaluation research," pp. 141-163 in C. H. Weiss (ed.) Using Social Research in Public Policy Making. Lexington, MA: Lexington-Heath.

PELZ, D. C. (1978) "Some expanded perspectives on use of social science in public policy," pp. 346-357 in J. M. Yinger and S. J. Cutler (eds.) Major Social Issues: A Multidisciplinary View. New York: Free Press.

REIN, M. and S. WHITE (1977) "Can policy research help policy?" Public Interest 49: 119-136.

RICH, R. F. (1977) "Use of social science information by Federal bureaucrats: Knowledge for action versus knowledge for understanding," pp. 199-211 in C. H. Weiss (ed.) Using Social Research in Public Policy Making. Lexington, MA: Lexington-Heath.

——— (1975) "The power of information." Ph.D. dissertation, University of Chicago.

——— and N. CAPLAN (1976) "Policy uses of social science knowledge and perspectives: Means/ends matching versus understanding." Presented at the OECD Conference on "Dissemination of economic and social development research results," Bogota, Colombia, June.

ROWBOTTOM, R., J. BALLE, S. CANG, M. DIXON, E. JAQUES, T. PACKWOOD, and H. TOLLIDAY (1973) Hospital Organization. London: Heineman.

SIMON, H. A. (1976) Administrative Behavior. New York: Free Press.

THOMPSON, J. D. (1967) Organizations in Action. New York: McGraw-Hill.

WEICK, K. E. (1969) The Social Psychology of Organizing. Reading, MA: Addison-Wesley.

WEISS, C. H. (1977) "Introduction," pp. 1-22 in C. H. Weiss (ed.) Using Social Research in Public Policy Making. Lexington, MA: Lexington-Heath.
––– (1970) The Consequences of the Study of Federal Student Loan Programs: A Case Study in the Utilization of Social Research. New York: Bureau of Applied Social Research.
WHITE, B. F. (1975) "The Atlanta project: How one large school system responded to performance information." Policy Analysis 1: 659-691.

2

ASSESSING EVALUATION UTILIZATION
IN HUMAN SERVICE AGENCIES

John F. Stevenson

University of Rhode Island

INTRODUCTION

When I started work as an apprentice evaluator in a psychiatric hospital, one of my first assignments was to "evaluate the evaluators." It is on the basis of this painful but interesting experience that I will discuss various issues and strategies for measuring the utilization of evaluation results in human service organizations. Although I turned to the literature for help in my efforts to assess evaluation effectiveness, I found that the context and role demands faced by local, internal, evaluators created special conditions not usually addressed in the literature. For this reason I went on to develop my own approach, involving the application of varying criteria for utilization as a function of the intended purpose of evaluation activities. In this article I will review the reasoning which led to my present position on utilization measurement and suggest some alternative approaches for application in the local setting.

The Insider Role

Weeks (1979) and Wholey (1972) have suggested that much of the potentially most useful evaluation goes on at the local service delivery level. Cohen (1977) has asserted that local policies are rarely affected by evaluation findings obtained in other settings. The present article takes the position that local evaluation is widespread, is already having an important influence on service delivery, and offers special challenges for utilization measurement.

From the perspective of the evaluator working within a local service delivery organization, the primary concern is with the utilization of evaluation results by management. Continuing employment, as well as status and power within the organization, are contingent on useful results. Other potential users of evaluation findings, such as service delivery staff, funding sources, the local citizenry, other similar organizations, and professional colleagues, take on greater or lesser importance depending on the nature of management's concerns. Evaluators, of course, can in turn attempt to influence their employers' expectations, but this must be done in the context of an established administrative hierarchy, rather than that of the autonomous professional entrepreneur selling services to a temporary client. Concern by internal evaluators for traditionally defined methodological rigor is also secondary to concern for utilization. Methodological rigor takes on importance to the extent that it increases the impact of findings by making them more credible and/or by imbuing them with the mystique of science. Responsiveness to administrative needs also accounts for the wide variety of evaluation techniques and formats which are likely to be employed by a single evaluator in a single setting. Descriptive data required by external funding sources, formative evaluation to improve programs, and summative evaluation to determine overall merit of programs are all part of the job.

Evaluators who work as employees of the organization they evaluate are often viewed as providing an internal "feedback loop" (Bigelow and Ciarlo, 1976; Etzioni, 1969; Katz, 1975; Schulberg and Baker, 1969). Their role may be "summative" for individual programs within the setting, but it is always "formative" for the organization as a whole. This ongoing relationship between organizational functioning and evaluation feedback provides an interesting context for examining the factors which affect utilization. The "insider" role has both advantages and disadvantages for the evaluator seeking to maximize utility. Cohen (1977) suggested that insiders are likely to be viewed as more trustworthy and sympathetic by program staff, but also as less expert and objective. Insiders are likely to have more qualitative knowledge of the process of service delivery, more direct and informal access to administrators, and more potential to take a long view of evaluation impact and to view themselves as resident change agents. Simultaneously, however, they are more vulnerable to the immediate concerns of administrators. Objective indices of utilization are more threatening but also more directly useful to the insider. The stable presence of the internal evaluator allows implementation of an ongoing feedback system for measuring the utilization of evaluation and for tracking the pattern of demand for evaluation. Opportunities to experiment with alternative strategies for maximizing utilization, such as early staff involvement, use of multiattribute utility theory (Edwards et al., 1975), to establish information needs, and various dissemination techniques are enhanced by the stable context. However, such experimentation may be viewed as a luxury by impatient administrators.

Since inside evaluators are already in relatively constant contact with users, and since their longevity in the setting allows them to observe the results of their work, it might seem superfluous to engage in systematic utilization measurement activities. In the author's experience, inside evaluators draw conclusions about the utilization of their work on the basis of verbalizations by administrators, new requests for evaluation, dramatic successes or failures of evaluation recommendations to produce intended decisions, evaluation budget fluctuations, and changes in their position and responsibilities within the organization. These kinds of feedback, while certainly pertinent, may not be sufficient. A temporal lag between an evaluation report and policy changes may obscure the relationship. Administrators may subtly communicate their wishes for changes in performance to program staff, never formally changing policies or acknowledging the role of evaluation findings. When there are multiple clients for an evaluation study, some may use the results while others do not. Verbal acceptance of findings may not be followed by appropriate action. Verbal rejection of findings may be followed by actions which imply acceptance. Despite general indications that their work is appreciated and in some cases very influential, evaluators may find such qualitative feedback too insensitive and imprecise to be confident about which of the evaluation and dissemination strategies they have employed maximize utilization. And they may question the relevance of utilization studies done in very different contexts. Bonoma (1977) has acknowledged that settings probably differ too much for any one formula to successfully promote utilization in all of them.

UTILIZATION CRITERIA

Background on Utilization Measurement in the Human Services

Although research on knowledge utilization is not new, very little attention has been given to problems of utilization measurement in the human services. Several authors have discussed means of improving the usefulness of evaluation findings in the human services, and measurement issues are implicit in some of these discussions. A few recent attempts have been made to measure utilization, and these provide a starting point for the development of new assessment techniques.

Formative versus Summative Approaches. In an important review and synthesis of the literature on evaluation utilization, Davis and Salasin (1975: 676) asserted that "better tracer evaluations of evaluation utilization itself would offer more reinforcement to evaluators." Citing support by Weiss and Ciarlo, Davis and Salasin advocated extended monitoring of evaluation impact as a means to detect effects masked by temporal lag. The notion that utilization measurement should be a formative shaping process carried out over an extended period of time can be contrasted with the notion that a single summative judgment of utilization is appropriate. The formative approach is also implicit in an earlier discussion by Schulberg and Baker (1969) of the applicability of a systems model to program evaluation in the health fields. Schulberg and Baker pointed out the value of studying the very feedback mechanisms which block or facilitate the application of evaluation findings. Despite the apparent value of the formative, temporally extended, process-oriented approach to utilization measurement, the approach taken in practice has been the large-N, single-time-sample one (e.g., Fairweather et al., 1974; Human Interaction Research Institute, 1976; Patton, 1978; Weeks, 1979).

Variation in Criteria. Another important question is whether a single set of criteria can appropriately be applied to measure utilization across context and purpose. I have already mentioned some of the special features of the evaluation context in local human service organizations, and more extended treatment of this topic may be found in Stevenson and Longabaugh (in press). There is substantial variation even within this type of organization, and one important source of such variation is the stage of development of the evaluation component within the organization (Hargreaves et al., 1975; Lund, 1978; McIntyre et al., 1977). Should the same criteria for utilization be applied to a fledgling client tracking system as to an experiment designed to test the relative cost-effectiveness of two alternative approaches to the treatment of alcohol problems? Similarly, when an evaluator is engaged in several very different types of evaluation activity intended to achieve very different purposes, are the same criteria appropriate for all? Murrell and Brown (1977: 275) argued that "To make an uncompromising judgment about any program evaluation effort, as well as a fair and realistic one, requires a clear recognition of the differences among the tasks, roles, and procedures of different categories of program evaluation efforts." Murrell and Brown went on to sketch separate criteria for three classes of evaluation activity. The first context for evaluation proposed by Murrell and Brown is the demonstration context, in which an evaluation is intended to establish reliable general causal relationships between variables. The appropriate criteria for such projects are those associated with scientific rigor, and direct utilization of the results is an unfair criterion to apply. The second of Murrell and Brown's contexts is program development, in which the purpose is to provide directly and immediately relevant information for program improvement, and the criterion is utilization by decision makers. The final context is account-ability, in which the purpose is to compel the program to conform to external standards, and the criteria concern the relevance and trustworthi-ness of the data for establishing whether the program is meeting its obligations.

Stevenson et al. (1978) have proposed a system for classifying evalua-tion purposes in terms of the type and location of impact sought. This system is in turn linked to alternative criteria for judging utilization, and these will be discussed below. It may often be uninformative and unrea-sonable to apply the same utilization criteria to evaluations of major federal programs and local program evaluation activities, to infant and fully mature evaluation enterprises, and to the several different kinds of evaluation activity which may be going on within a setting.

The Means-Ends Continuum: Utility versus Utilization. In a relatively early article on the utilization of evaluation, Halpert (1969) suggested that a good way to judge the effectiveness of the communication of an evaluation research finding would be to look for altered behavior of the clients for the evaluation. Fairweather et al. (1974) investigated the factors which predicted eventual adoption of a new program which had been empirically demonstrated to be effective. They found that behavioral commitment by administrators was more likely to be followed by adop-tion than was verbal commitment. In both of these cases, the emphasis was on observable actions by administrators as evidence for utilization of evaluation.

Cohen (1977) has suggested a continuum of possible goals for utiliza-tion impact, including (1) awareness of results by administrators, (2) con-sideration of results during decision making, (3) a resultant policy con-sistent with evaluation findings, and (4) diffusion to other settings. Cohen selected the second of these goals as most sensible, reasoning that there are too many other salient influences on policy decisions for evaluation findings to be "automatically converted into program policy."

The present article takes the position, described earlier by Stevenson et al. (1979), that measurable managerial behavior and organizational changes are the best indication of *utilization* of evaluation findings. Conceptions of *utility* which focus on the scientific merit of a study's methodology, the potential amount of information conveyed, lack of bias in reporting, timeliness, and relevance to the decision at hand all deal with the means rather than the ends of evaluation.

There are some good reasons why many discussions of evaluation impact have concentrated on utility rather than utilization. For one thing, influential writers on metaevaluation have appeared to believe that evaluators' responsibility extends only as far as the scientific rigor of their work (Cook and Gruder, 1978). In discrete studies of major social programs conducted by outside evaluators, this conception of evaluator-as-scientist is a tenable one and sets familiar limits on evaluators' responsibility. As I have already pointed out, the local inside evaluator is in a position to view evaluation as a continuous cyclic process, moving from planning to implementation, analysis, feedback of findings to administrators, administrative actions, organizational changes, and feedback to evaluators. If evaluators' responsibility is restricted to the phases of this cycle culminating in a written report, then evidence for utility of evaluation is easily accessible because evaluators need not look beyond their own activities. Although ease of access helps to account for focus on utility rather than utilization, it seems clear that administrative action and organizational change do lend themselves to empirical study and are in this sense well-suited to be criteria. By contrast, Cohen's (1977: 528) "consideration of evaluation research as one of several information inputs examined during a decision-making process" is a far more subjective criterion, though more in keeping with the evaluator-as-scientist concept.

Another possible reason for emphasis on assessment of utility rather than utilization is the difficulty of dealing with unintended evaluation consequences. Administrators may act on the basis of misunderstanding of evaluation results; the major uses of evaluation may be covert; organizational changes in response to evaluation may be unintended and fortuitous. In such cases it is problematic to define and measure utilization. It seems clear that limits must be placed on the kinds of administrative and organizational responses to evaluation which will be considered utilization. For example, an administrator may use evaluation as a weapon to harass a program director, leading to resignation by the program director and a realignment of the program's policy when a new director is hired. In this case the informational value of evaluation findings, and the recommendations in the final report, are relevant, at best, as a public statement of what has been widely known already. Another example is the case in which program staff's knowledge that they are being evaluated leads to change in organizational performance long before the data have been analyzed and reported (e.g., Rosenfield and Orlinsky, 1961). Situations like these represent unintended (at least by the evaluator) responses to evaluation. Assessment of utility, rather than utilization, appears to offer an escape from the responsibility for dealing with these important but unintended consequences. The escape comes at a very high price, though, which this author believes is not worth paying.

A final difficulty with measuring utilization, which makes it tempting to focus on utility, is that several potential users may wish to make use of the same evaluation. This is relatively common in internally conducted evaluations of local service delivery organizations. Under these conditions, some clients may utilize the results while others do not. In order to arrive at a single measure of utilization, choices must be made about how to identify a primary client or how to aggregate the various kinds and amounts of utilization by all important clients.

Despite difficulties in measuring actual utilization of evaluation findings, the argument in favor of doing so is straightforward. Evaluators in local settings are concerned not with potential utility but with administrative decisions and organizational changes resulting from their work. Weeks (1979) found that the methodological rigor of local evaluation projects was negatively correlated with evaluators' subjective estimates of actual impact. Brown et al. (1978) found that the amount of jargon and the amount of objective data in an evaluation report did not significantly affect ratings of the evaluator's credibility or agreement with the report's findings. Indeed, the jargon-free subjective report was rated most convincing, though not significantly different from the others. Findings like these support the need for research on factors associated with actual impact, since they challenge some versions of accepted wisdom about utility. A limited analogy may be drawn with research on mental health programs. Many early evaluation activities focused on the delivery of appropriate types and levels of care to appropriate client populations. Increasingly, emphasis has been placed on the measurement of actual client outcomes. This is particularly well-justified in a situation where the technology is still youthful and the links between methods and outcome are uncertain. Evaluation utilization is just such an area.

MEASUREMENT OF UTILIZATION

Current Measures of Utilization

Efforts to measure utilization in local human service settings are in their infancy. Most empirical approaches have relied on mailed surveys of evaluators and/or administrators, calling for subjective estimates of utilization (e.g., Weeks, 1979; Windle and Volkman, 1973). Other approaches include partially structured interviews with evaluation clients and/or evaluators (e.g., Bigelow and Ciarlo, 1976; Patton, 1978) and direct observation of program adoption by change agents (e.g., Fairweather et al., 1974).

I will describe one measure of utilization which was not oriented primarily toward local service delivery programs because it has received such wide attention. Patton (1978), along with some students, surveyed a sample of federally sponsored evaluations of health-related programs. Of 20 studies in the sample, 6 were conducted by inside evaluators and 14 by external evaluators. Decision makers and evaluators for each project were asked two open-ended questions about utilization in the course of a long tape-recorded interview (Patton, 1978: 27). One question was: "From your point of view, what was the impact of this evaluation study on the program we've been discussing?" The other was: "Did the evaluation have an impact on these [broader, more general] kinds of things?" A substantial majority of all of those interviewed answered in the affirmative to both questions. Evaluators saw more evidence of immediate program impact, while decision makers were more able to see longer term indirect impacts. Patton went on to develop a model for "utilization-focused" evaluation which postulates that evaluations are likely to be used to the extent that they increase the power of the user, and that the user's power will be increased to the extent that evaluation findings "reduce the uncertainty of action for specific decision-makers" (Patton, 1978: 50). He drew an analogy between the cognitive processes of the individual dealing with an environment full of causal ambiguity and the decision maker using evaluation findings to reduce uncertainty (i.e., to increase predictability of and control over the environment). Emphasis on identification of an individual client, on the role of this client's personal commitment to evaluation, and on the need for minimum organizational distance between client and evaluator all confirm the observations of others. And despite the caution which must be exercised in generalizing from Patton's findings to the local service delivery level, his recommendations appear very relevant. However, his elegant attempt to define utilization in terms of uncertainty reduction (not apparent in his own interview measure) presents problems which will be discussed below.

Two other approaches to utilization measurement have relied on mailed surveys directed to large samples of local evaluation sites. Windle and Volkman (1973) surveyed federally funded community mental health centers and asked about utilization in terms of specific program changes resulting from all of their evaluation activities. Subjective reports by managers indicated that 70% of the responding centers had made use of evaluation for changing programs, and 52% of the changes were in the direction of program expansion or the addition of new programs. Only 8% of the changes were in the direction of reduction or elimination of programs. Findings at this level of abstraction are not useful for formative shaping of evaluation efforts, and subjective responses by managers may not be trustworthy. The request for a list of specific program changes does have merit as a means of objectifying managers' responses.

Weeks (1979), in the most thorough study to date, used a mail survey questionnaire with a large sample of "local implementations of social programs conducted within California between 1975 and 1977." Evaluators rated utilization on a 10-point scale. The lowest rating was: "Most of the decision participants probably didn't even read the report. Nobody considered that it could tell them much they didn't already know." The highest rating was: "Many of the recommendations were adopted and implemented. In that sense, the evaluation study effectively made the program decisions." The psychometric properties of the scale were acceptable, and it appears useful as a global, ordinal, subjective measure of utilization. As Weeks pointed out, asking evaluators to rate the utilization of their products is a measurement method vulnerable to response bias problems. Validation of the scale against other measures of utilization, such as independent reports by administrators, would have greatly increased the impact of Weeks's findings. Another problem with this scale is that in some cases evaluation studies may have achieved their desired impact and yet received only a moderate rating. For example, a rating of six is defined by the phrase: "The evaluation study definitely had a major impact in indicating to the decision participants what needed improvement but the study was not used significantly in deciding how to achieve the improvement." In a scale development procedure this item was lowest in agreement on its rank order. Problem identification may be the ultimate purpose of some evaluation studies, and impact of this kind may be viewed by evaluators and decision makers as representing high utilization when this is the purpose of the study.

A number of innovation diffusion studies have operationalized utilization as a dichotomous dependent variable: adoption versus nonadoption. Fairweather et al. (1974) provide a good example of this approach to the study of utilization, as do a number of the studies abstracted in a report by the Human Interaction Research Institute (1976). In some cases, attention has been paid to the degree of congruity between the program as recommended and the program as implemented, though this has generally been done in a qualitative way. Such studies, and particularly that of Fairweather and his associates, offer some intriguing observations on the factors associated with utilization. However, innovation diffusion is a different undertaking from that ordinarily engaged in by local program evaluators, and empirical study will be necessary to verify the usefulness of these observations for the inside evaluator.

Bigelow and Ciarlo (1976) came closest to the perspective of the local evaluator when they studied the impact of two evaluation reports on community mental health center managers. In the part of their study which examined the actual impact of specific findings, a questionnaire was administered to managers immediately following oral presentation of evaluation findings, and a follow-up interview was conducted three weeks later. The questionnaire investigated comprehension of the report and intentions for action. The follow-up interview queried congruity of the data with prior impressions, subsequent actions, other influences on actions, and further information which would provide useful feedback on actions taken. The results helped to identify sources of confusion in the communication process, links between intentions and actions, mediating factors, and targets for further study. As the authors pointed out, their design intruded into the ongoing utilization process and may very well have affected that process. Only two evaluation projects were studied, making the results most useful as qualitative case studies rather than as quantitative approaches to utilization measurement. The open-ended questions provided a minimum of structure and necessitated relatively unsophisticated quantification.

To summarize, efforts to measure evaluation utilization in local service delivery organizations have, for the most part, sampled across settings, examined the impact of a single evaluation, and relied on subjective reports by evaluators or decision makers. From a systems perspective, a more useful direction for future inquiry would be to extend the work of Bigelow and Ciarlo (1976), sampling over an extended time period within a setting with more precise and objective measures of utilization. This would allow clarification of the role of many factors, such as staff involvement, report style, timing, design rigor, personalization, and so on, which have been identified in other contexts as contributing to utilization.

Future Directions

How can the impact of evaluation activities on service delivery be understood and improved in the local setting? It has been suggested here that, like managers and service delivery personnel, internal evaluators need reliable, objective, ongoing feedback on their effectiveness. Like managers and service staff, they are entitled to a little defensiveness about this kind of feedback, and that should be taken into acount in efforts to design utilization measures. A longitudinal, formative approach and development of tailored, purpose-specific criteria seem appropriate means of providing constructive feedback. Despite difficulties in precisely defining utilization, evaluators need to know how managerial decisions and organizational behavior have actually been affected by their work. Approaches which focus on the potential utility of evaluation, or which rely on subjective, global estimates of impact, are less informative.

Uncertainty Reduction. One implication of the discussion above is that a relatively precise and objective measure of utilization would be a great boon. Patton (1978: 50) has seemingly laid the groundwork for such a measure by defining impact in terms of "uncertainty reduction."This term has a technical meaning within information theory (Attneave, 1959; Garner, 1962) which could be used to develop an operational definition. In developing his position, Patton noted some limits on his conception of information as power: (1) not all information is useful and (2) not all people are information users. These limitations are serious ones for an approach which Patton (1978: 57) characterized as "not aimed merely at potential utilization but rather at actual utilization." Later in his book, Patton (1978: 289-290) apparently obviated these limitations by denying that utilization should be defined in terms of behavioral change and reasserting the virtues of "information capable of reducing uncertainty." There seems to be some ambiguity in Patton's definition of a criterion for utilization. The difficulty may lie in Patton's belief that the most important type of utilization is "conceptual" (Rich, 1976), that is, indirect and cumulative, rather than immediate and decisive ("instrumental" in Rich's terms).

Since "uncertainty reduction" does have a technical meaning which might make it a good candidate for an operational definition of utilization, I will present my own reasons for not favoring this approach. In doing so, I will be extending some of Patton's criticisms.

Application of information theory presumes that the decision maker starts with a set of prior probability estimates for a series of possible causal relationships or states of affairs. An example might be: "The probability that this program is accomplishing its stated objective is .7; the probability that it is not doing so is .3." The evaluation reduces uncertainty by clarifying which state of affairs is actually the case, or which state of affairs would obtain if a particular action were taken by the decision maker, ideally determining that one state of affairs is 100% probable. Mathematically, the degree of uncertainty reduction is a log function of the amount of change in prior probabilities contributed by the evaluation findings. Thus, a possible state of affairs (or decision outcome) with relatively low prior probability (in the view of the administrator), if confirmed as the actual state of affairs by research, leads to greater uncertainty reduction than the confirmation of a hypothesis which was already viewed as highly probable. Sometimes "information" is defined as the actual amount of uncertainty reduction which has been accomplished (after the results are in). At other times, informational value is calculated on the basis of potential uncertainty reduction (when only the prior probabilities are known). In the latter case, the greatest informational value obtains when all possible outcomes are equally probable. For a situation with two possible outcomes (e.g., the program is, or is not, accomplishing its primary objective), maximum *potential* uncertainty reduction would exist if the prior probability of each outcome were .5. The following discussion will generally assume the first definition given above, rather than the second.

There are several difficulties with this approach to utilization measurement. First of all, if it is decision makers whose uncertainty is to be reduced, then it is their probability estimates which are important. Evaluators may view their results as supporting conclusions which greatly reduce uncertainty, but if this information is misunderstood, not believed, or viewed as a replication of known facts by the decision maker, then whatever potential utility for uncertainty reduction the results may have is not being realized. Patton acknowledged this problem. To measure genuine uncertainty reduction, as distinguished from potential uncertainty reduction, we need to know the prior and posterior probabilities attached by decision makers to the range of options they view as possible. In many cases this may call for a degree of candor on the part of decision makers which may put a strain on their relationships with evaluators. The point I am making here is closely related to my earlier discussion of the contrast between potential utility and actual utilization.

A second difficulty with the use of uncertainty reduction as a means of quantifying utilization is that it appears most likely for evaluation results to be taken seriously when they confirm prior impressions or are consistent with other concurrent sources of evidence. Remember that uncertainty reduction is a function of amount of change in prior probabilities, not a measure of confidence. If uncertainty reduction is negatively related to plausibility, one might conclude that utility is inversely related to utilization. Patton (1978) himself provided examples of the confirmatory role evaluation results often play. Ellsworth (1975) discussed, and gave good case illustrations of, the tendency of decision makers to stick to their preexisting perceptions despite disconfirming evidence. Cochran (1978) and Scriven (1975) also pointed out the difficulties in using evaluation data to override the existing commitments and biases of decision makers. Windle (1976) interpreted the data presented in Windle and Volkman (1973) as evidence that program administrators make use of evaluation results which confirm the need for continuation or expansion of programs more than they make use of results which call for reduction or elimination of programs. Bigelow and Ciarlo (1976) provided another example of the underutilization of improbable findings. Up to a point, it is *redundancy* rather than uncertainty reduction which enhances the prospects for utilization. This reasoning suggests that in practice, objective informational value (amount of uncertainty reduction) is inversely related to utilization. Empirical investigation of this question is clearly called for.

A third difficulty is that the set of possible states of affairs with which the decision maker starts may be expanded by evaluation results. Decision makers generally must make simplifying assumptions about the range of possible options which can be considered. For example, an administrator might be trying to decide whether to increase the budget for a struggling new program or to discontinue the program and divert the funds to other ongoing operations. The evaluator is asked: "Which of these two options is preferable?" The eventual report might conclude that the cost per client is higher in this program, that the clients have special needs which are not being addressed elsewhere, that the recidivism rates (or other outcome measures) are comparable to those in other programs when certain intake characteristics are covaried, that some clients are entering the program whose problems are not ameliorated by it, and that certain components of the program appear most effective. An answer like this seems eminently useful, but it does not reduce the administrator's uncertainty with regard to the initial question. It expands the range of options. The point here is that decision makers may have uncertainties created that they did not start out with. This can lead to a state of information overload, in which the decision maker relies on other, less complex considerations when making the decision at hand and no longer seeks the optimal choice.

To extend the preceding point, it may sometimes be the case that evaluators desire to *increase* the uncertainty of administrators. This seems particularly likely to occur when decision makers favor the status quo and expect evaluators to provide feedback useful for maintaining equilibrium. Evaluators, inspired by reading about the "change agent" role, as well as by their own values, may attempt to expand administrators' set of possible options. Once a state of expanded awareness of alternative realities has been inculcated, evaluators may be able to conduct studies which reduce uncertainty once more, but the initial increase seems a useful impact of evaluation under some conditions.

As a model for utilization measurement, information theory appears to have limited but interesting potential. Specification of the relationship between informational value and utilization under various conditions seems a worthwhile undertaking. As a criterion for utilization it may be applicable under certain circumstances, but not always. This point leads the discussion back to the position that utilization criteria should vary according to the intended impact of the study and that the evaluation-dissemination-utilization chain should be studied as a cyclic process.

The Internal Evaluation System. My initial response to a request to evaluate an evaluation division within a psychiatric hospital was to develop a model of the ongoing evaluation process and its interfaces with the rest of the organization. It was in the context of this model that I began to plan utilization measurement activities. I started by crystallizing my informal observations of the evaluation process into a flow chart. Ranged along the top of the flow chart were the steps in a typical evaluation project, from initial request or inspiration, through several phases of planning and implementation, to dissemination. Down the left margin were listed various kinds of personnel from inside and outside the division. For each of a randomly selected set of evaluation reports completed in the past year, I asked several key personnel to indicate the timing and staff involvement for the entire evaluation process. In addition to discovering intriguing differences of opinion—particularly about the initial impetus for projects—I was able to discern several different standard patterns which were associated with different types of evaluation activity. The next step was to extend the flow chart into managerial and organizational responses to evaluations similar to those proposed by Cohen (1978). Client attention, comprehension, acceptance, weighting, and action were added, followed by staff implementation and performance change.

On the basis of this conceptual model, several observations were made possible. First, the completion of the cycle requires feedback to evaluators which may come at any or all of the points following dissemination. Utilization measurement in this context is a means of providing more precise, objective, and timely feedback to evaluators from these various postdissemination points. Second, the patterns reflected in the flow chart of evaluation planning, implementation, and dissemination are likely to affect the amount and type of utilization. Third, the most appropriate kinds of feedback on utilization vary as a function of the nature and purpose of evaluation projects. Fourth, some phases of utilization lend themselves to objective measurement while others do not. Specifically, client acceptance and weighting require relatively subjective measurement strategies, and long-term "conceptual" (Rich, 1976) or "understanding-relevant" (Bennett and Lumsdaine, 1975) kinds of utilization are difficult to estimate in any but the most subjective of ways.

Purpose-Specific Criteria. Elsewhere this author has proposed that the desired impacts of evaluation in local service delivery settings can be classified into a two-dimensional framework (Stevenson et al., 1979). Figure 1 presents a slightly modified typology based on this framework and also lists a series of stages in utilization. For each type of intended evaluation impact, there are appropriate subjective, and in some cases objective, indications of utilization. Five general classes of evaluation activity, based on intended impact, are listed and briefly described below.

When a *major internal decision* regarding the future of a program is the objective of an evaluation activity, the evaluator is likely to strive to undertake a formal study, relatively summative, including measures of outcome and costs. Pains may be taken to approximate an experimental design and to maximize internal validity. The report may often resemble a research article for a journal, though in an expanded form. Major program changes are explicitly at stake. An example of this kind of evaluation is a study of an innovative inpatient treatment program for persons with alcohol problems, comparing costs and outcomes with preexisting normal treatment options. In this case the clients for the evaluation (a third-party

FIGURE 1: Criteria for Potential Utility and Utilization, Applied to Varying Evaluation Objectives

Typology of Evaluation Objectives	Potential Utility Critera							Utilization Criteria						
	Reliable measures	Internal validity	External validity	Relevance to needs	Clarity implications	Timeless	Information value	Attention	Comprehension	Acceptance	Weighting	Congruent decision action	Implementation/Adoption	Program performance
I. Major internal decisions	X	X		X	X	X	X	X	X	X	X	X		
II. Procedural changes	X			X	X	X		X	X	X	X			X
III. Equilibrium maintenance	X			X	X			X	X	X	X	X	X	X
IV. Planning														
A. Short-term	X			X	X	X	X	X	X	X	X	X		
B. Long-term	X	X					X	X	X	X	X			
V. External dissemination	X	X	X	X	X			X	X	X	X	X	X	

*If the data indicate problems requiring action; the action might well be a focused evaluation study.

payer and hospital administrators) explicitly planned to expand or terminate the program and expected the research results to aid in the decision. The results were ambiguous; the report went into detail about methodological shortcomings; the program was redesigned; and a new, methodologically improved study was commissioned. Criteria for utilization of this kind of evaluation extend to congruous policy decisions. The example illustrates the necessity of distinguishing utilization from potential utility. Given the potential, the study was well-utilized. Both evaluators and administrators can make judgments about the factors associated with potential utility, and their perceptions can be compared. The best sources of data about actual utilization are the subjective reports of administrators and more objective evidence, such as policy statements.

The author developed two measurement strategies which are relevant for this type of evaluation. For all evaluation reports issued in a three-year period, a list of explicit policy recommendations and clear policy implications was compiled. Next, all formal policy statements released during that time were reviewed. Policy changes were linked to evaluation reports with which they were consistent. Graphic representations indicated "hit-rate" per quarter and lag-time per study. One planned extension of this approach is a technique for rating the magnitude of policy changes.

The second relevant measurement strategy is a pair of questionnaires, parallel in form, which call for evaluators and administrators to describe a particular evaluation, indicating its purpose, its potential for utility, and its actual utilization. Items are worded as specifically and concretely as possible to avoid global judgments. Questions are grouped according to evaluation purpose, so that only criteria relevant to actual purposes are rated by respondents. Only preliminary use has been made of these questionnaires, but they offer promise of providing subjective indications of rigor, timeliness, relevance, attention, comprehensibility, credibility (acceptance), relative weighting, and administrative action. Comparison of the perceptions of evaluators and administrators may be instructive. Validation against records of policy decisions is planned.

A second type of evaluation activity is intended to culminate in *specific procedural recommendations,* but not in radical program alteration or elimination. The orientation is formative, and the data focus on process, though outcome data may be used as well. Such an evaluation is likely to be undertaken with explicit acknowledgment that there seem to be some problems, and there is need for guidance about how to improve things. An example is a study of a specialized acute care unit in a psychiatric hospital which was undertaken in response to indications that formal policy regarding brief treatment and rapid transfer to less costly care was no longer being followed and that staff organization on the unit might be weakening. The intent of the study was to scrutinize the admission and release processes, to observe staff interaction, and to obtain anonymous data on staff perceptions of organizational climate. Collaboration with unit staff in the development of instruments led to clarifications of procedures, and recommendations for ways of tightening admissions and loosening transfers were put into effect.

Appropriate utilization criteria for this kind of evaluation do not include evidence of major policy decisions, but do include administrative acceptance of recommendations and measurable changes in organizational performance. Evidence for potential utility does not extend to experimental rigor, but does include reliability and absence of bias in measures, explicitness of recommendations, and relevance of recommendations to acknowledged problems. In addition to the questionnaires described earlier, utilization measurement can take the form of continued monitoring of appropriate performance indices and restudy. In this case restudy is not intended to establish the accuracy of the original findings by replicating them, but rather to test for change in the desired direction.

An obvious flaw in the several "objective" indications of utilization I have proposed—policy change tabulation, performance monitoring, and restudy—is that they may fluctuate in response to factors other than evaluation reports. In an "experimenting society" a series of evaluation utilization studies might be conducted in which control settings muddled through without evaluation or with alternative evaluation strategies. In the present world, local evaluators may be able to achieve moderate confidence in the nature of their impact by using several independent means of measuring utilization simultaneously and by examining administrative action and organizational performance in a time series perspective. Converging evidence that evaluation reports carry meaningful weight in decisions, and discontinuities in performance which coincide with evaluation feedback, should help in this regard.

A third type of evaluation activity is intended to provide *periodic feedback* of a descriptive sort about indices of organizational performance which are seen by administrators as useful in maintaining equilibrium and quality of service delivery. The data are descriptive, plotted over time, and may include both process and outcome measures, although the former are more common. Specific recommendations are not expected, but identification of performance problems is. An example of this kind of evaluation activity is a quarterly report in a psychiatric setting which presents current statistics on median length of treatment, usage of major medications, admitting problems, service usage, and so on, in the context of temporal patterns. It was a report of this sort which helped to identify the difficulties of the acute care unit described in the preceding example, and similar reports have documented the impact of changes in policy, the advent of new programs, the cyclic nature of some phenomena, and so on. Utilization criteria are restricted to comprehension and acceptance of the report unless administrative action is called for. Potential utility resides in reliable and unbiased measures, relevance of indices for administrative concerns, and clarity of the report. Of particular concern to local evaluators are cases where administrators fail to notice evidence of organizational performance decrements which appear to call for action and cases where administrators overinterpret minor fluctuations. The utilization questionnaires provide the best evidence for most of these criteria.

A fourth type of evaluation activity is intended for *planning purposes*. Information for planning can be focused on short-term assessment of needs and resources or it can be oriented toward a long-term increase in conceptual understanding of the causal relationships which future decisions may have to take into account. An example of evaluation oriented toward future planning potential is a study of the characteristics of care-providing teams which were associated with better client outcomes. This study was not directed at an immediate decision need, but provided potentially useful knowledge about team structure and process. Another example is a correlational study of organizational indices to identify "early warning" indicators of disequilibrium. Utilization of short-term planning-relevant input can be measured in the same ways that apply to decision-relevant evaluation. Long-term conceptually focused input calls for high standards of internal validity, plus administrative comprehension and acceptance. Unlike the case for short-term planning, objective measures of managerial action are inappropriate for this conceptually oriented type of evaluation, as Patton (1978: 289-290) has pointed out. Internally valid conceptual knowledge need have no immediate application to be of long-term use. However, research of this kind is relatively rare in local service delivery organizations, as is the following kind.

A fifth type of evaluation activity is the *classic demonstration project*. Although the data may be used for local purposes as well, the major focus is on demonstrating the effectiveness of an innovative program, so that it can be adopted with confidence in other settings. Utilization criteria in this case are straightforward: Positive findings should receive the attention of potential adopters, should be understood and believed, should be given substantial weight in decisions about growth and change, and should lead to adoption. Criteria for potential utility include the design considerations for both internal and external validity, relevance to current concerns in potential adopting organizations, and clarity of report. Survey question-naires or interviews can be used to assess all of these criteria. Validity concerns can also be addressed through the variety of more objective means described by Cook and Gruder (1978). The similarity of imple-mented programs to the pilot program, an important concern, would be difficult to measure in other than a subjective fashion.

For the local evaluator, the foregoing approach offers a mix of qualita-tive and quantitative means for gaining more precise and objective indica-tions of evaluation utilization. Patterns of utilization over time, and differences among evaluation activities employing alternative strategies, are potential findings which can be used in the formative shaping of the evaluation and dissemination process.

CONCLUSION

The assertion which ties most of the ideas in this article together was stated at the outset: Internal evaluators in local service delivery organiza-tions are primarily focused on meeting the needs of managers. Efforts to maximize the utilization of their work are of obvious importance to local evaluators for this reason, but there are also some important risks in such an orientation. Emphasizing utilization under such conditions may appear to make evaluators into slaves of management. Hastily collected data, used when it allows cost-cutting, expansion of pet programs, or preservation of the status quo, and ignored when it does not, must not be allowed to become the chief result from efforts to increase utilization. Evaluators must not embrace the role of managerial "enforcer" if they wish to preserve credibility with service delivery personnel. Despite these risks, an active, collaborative role with managerial decision makers still seems to offer the most promising context for meaningful evaluation activities.

At this point the question is not *whether* evaluation is utilized, but what kind of evaluation problems addressed with what evaluation strate-gies produce what sort of utilization. To provide answers to this which are generalizable beyond a single setting will require aggregation at the regional or national level. Combining the results of a series of studies conducted at the local level offers promise of being more relevant and generalizable than national surveys of selected evaluation projects or a demonstration project. As I discovered in my own attempt to assess utilization and identify the factors which affect it, the process is too complex for the application of a single utilization criterion across purposes and role contexts. This article has argued that a fruitful understanding of utilization can most readily be gained when it is viewed as part of an ongoing evaluation system which includes input requests for evaluation, planning, data collection, analysis, reporting, and a series of administrative and organizational responses which can provide feedback to the evaluator.

REFERENCES

ATTNEAVE, F. (1959) Applications of Information Theory to Psychology: A Summary of Basic Concepts, Methods, and Results. New York: Holt, Rinehart and Winston.

BENNETT, C. A. and A. A. LUMSDAINE (1975) "Social program evaluation: Definitions and issues," in C. A. Bennett and A. A. Lumsdaine (eds.) Evaluation and Experiment. New York: Academic Press.

BIGELOW, D. A. and J. A. CIARLO (1976) "The impact of therapeutic effectiveness data on community mental health center management," in G. V. Glass (ed.) Evaluation Studies Review Annual (Vol. 1). Beverly Hills, CA: Sage.

BONOMA, T. V. (1977) "Overcoming resistance to changes recommended for operating programs." Professional Psychology 8: 526-534.

BROWN, R. D., L. A. BRASKAMP, and D. L. NEWMAN (1978) "Evaluation credibility as a function of report style." Evaluation Quarterly 2: 331-341.

COCHRAN, N. (1978) "Cognitive processes, social mores, and the accumulation of data." Evaluation Quarterly 2: 343-358.

COHEN, L. H. (1977) "Factors affecting the utilization of mental health evaluation research findings." Professional Psychology 8: 526-534.

COOK, T. D. and C. L. GRUDER (1978) "Metaevaluation research." Evaluation Quarterly 2: 5-51.

DAVIS, H. R. and S. E. SALASIN (1975) "The utilization of evaluation," in E. L. Struening and M. Guttentag (eds.) Handbook of Evaluation Research (Vol. 1). Beverly Hills, CA: Sage.

EDWARDS, W., M. GUTTENTAG, and K. SNAPPER (1975) "A decision-theoretic approach to evaluation research," in E. L. Struening and M. Guttentag (eds.) Beverly Hills, CA: Sage.

ELLSWORTH, R. B. (1975) "Consumer feedback in measuring the effectiveness of mental health programs," in M. Guttentag and E. L. Struening (eds.) Handbook of Evaluation Research (Vol. 2). Beverly Hills, CA: Sage.

ETZIONI, A. (1969) "Two approaches to organizational analysis: A critique and a suggestion," in H. C. Schulberg et al. (eds.) Program Evaluation in the Health Fields. New York: Behavioral Publications.

FAIRWEATHER, G. W., D. H. SANDERS, and L. G. TORNATZKY (1974) Creating Change in Mental Health Organizations. New York: Pergamon.

GARNER, W. R. (1962) Uncertainty and Structure as Psychological Concepts. New York: John Wiley.

HALPERT, H. H. (1969) "Communications as a basic tool in promoting utilization of research findings," in H. C. Schulberg et al. (eds.) Program Evaluation in the Health Fields. New York: Behavioral Publications.

HARGREAVES, W. A., C. C. ATKISSON, M. H. McINTYRE, and L. M. SIEGEL (1975) "Current applications of evaluation," pp. 181-190 in J. Zusman and C. R. Wurster (eds.) Program Evaluation. Lexington, MA: Lexington Books.

Human Interaction Research Institute (1976) Putting Knowledge to Use: A Distillation of the Literature Regarding Knowledge Transfer and Change. Washington, DC: Government Printing Office.

KATZ, D. (1975) "Feedback in social systems: Operational and systemic research on production maintenance, control, and adaptive functions," pp. 465-523 in C. A. Bennet and A. A. Lumsdaine (eds.) Evaluation and Experiment. New York: Academic Press.

LUND, D. A. (1978) "Mental health program evaluation: Where you start?" Evaluation and Program Planning 1: 31-40.

McINTYRE, M. H., C. C. ATKISSON, and T. W. KELLER (1977) "Components of program evaluation capability in community mental health centers," in W. A. Hargreaves et al. (eds.) Resource Materials for Community Mental Health Program Evaluation (DHEW Publication No. ADM77-328). Washington, DC: Government Printing Office.

MURRELL, S. A. and F. BROWN (1977) "Judging program evaluations: Criteria in contexts," in R. D. Coursey et al. (eds.) Program Evaluation for Mental Health. New York: Grune and Stratton.

PATTON, M. Q. (1978) Utilization-Focused Evaluation. Beverly Hills, CA: Sage.

RICH, R. F. (1976) Uses of social science information by federal bureaucrats: Knowledge for action versus knowledge for understanding. Presented at the Annual Meeting of the Midwest Political Science Association, Chicago, April 29-May 1.

ROSENFIELD, J. M. and N. ORLINSKY (1961) "The effects of research on practice: Research and decrease in noncontinuance" Archives of General Psychiatry 5: 176-182.

SCHULBERG, H. C. and F. BAKER (1969) "Program evaluation models and the implementation of research findings," pp. 562-572 in H. C. Schulberg et al. (eds.) Program Evaluation in the Health Fields. New York: Behavioral Publications.

SCRIVEN, M. S. (1975) Evaluation Bias and Its Control. Kalamazoo: Western Michigan University, Evaluation Center.

STEVENSON, J. F. and R. H. LONGABAUGH (forthcoming) "The role of evaluation in mental health." Evaluation Review.

——— and D. N. McNEILL (1979) "Meta-evaluation in the human services," pp. 37-54 in H. C. Schulberg and J. M. Jerrell (eds.) The Evaluator and Management. Beverly Hills, CA: Sage.

WEEKS, E. (1979) "Factors affecting the utilization of evaluation at the local level: An empirical test," pp. 137-155 in H. C. Schulberg and J. M. Jerrell (eds.) The Evaluator and Management. Beverly Hills, CA: Sage.

WHOLEY, J. S. (1972) "What can we actually get from program evaluation?" Policy Sciences 3: 361-369.

WINDLE, C. (1976) "A crisis for program evaluation: An embarrassment of opportunity." Presented at the Region I Program Evaluation Conference, Providence, Rhode Island.

——— and E. M. VOLKMAN (1973) "Evaluation in the centers program." Evaluation 1(2): 69-70.

3

MEASURING EVALUATION UTILIZATION:
A Critique of Different Techniques

Ross F. Conner

University of California, Irvine

Evaluation research, unlike other social research, is meant to be used more or less immediately and directly in improving social policy and social programs. In part, the rise in the amount and prominence of evaluation research in the late 1960s and early 1970s can be attributed to studies at that time which documented the low degree of utilization of social research in policy making and program improvement (e.g., U.S. House of Representatives, Committee on Governmental Operations, 1967; National Academy of Sciences, 1968; Special Commission on the Social Sciences, National Science Foundation, 1968; Social Science Research Council, 1969). The results of these and more recent studies (e.g., Wholey et al., 1971; Goodwin, 1975; Hargrove, 1975; Deitchman, 1976) have demonstrated the importance and necessity of studying the utilization process.

The central question, consequently, is no longer, "Should we study utilization?" but instead is, "How do we study utilization?" The purpose of this article is to provide an answer—or rather, different possible answers—to this question. In the section that follows, I will describe and analyze eight studies of utilization. My focus, however, will not be on the results of these studies. Instead, this article will focus on a detailed description and analysis of the different techniques and approaches the

AUTHOR'S NOTE: An earlier version of this article was presented at the Evaluation Research Society Annual Meeting, Minneapolis, Minnesota, October 17-20, 1979.

eight studies used. Those readers interested in factors affecting the degree of utilization can consult other relevant studies (e.g., Argyris, 1965; Bennis et al., 1976; Bernstein and Freeman, 1975; Caplan et al., 1975; Chester and Flanders, 1967; Coe and Bernhill, 1967; Davis and Salasin, 1975; Fairweather, 1967; Fairweather et al., 1974; Glaser and Taylor, 1973, Havelock, 1969; Human Interaction Research Institute and National Institute of Mental Health, 1976; Weiss, 1972, 1977).

STUDIES OF UTILIZATION

The studies reviewed below are drawn primarily from a sample of quantitative investigations of research use identified by Weiss and Bucuvalas (1977: 229). Investigators from each of the studies were contacted for detailed information on the methodology they had employed to research utilization. These materials were reviewed for information on samples, measurement, methods, reliability figures, and the like. The study descriptions which follow present all of the methodological details which were available on each study.

The Weiss and Bucuvalas Study

This utilization study (Weiss and Bucuvalas, 1977; Weiss and Bucuvalas, forthcoming) assessed the characteristics of social science research studies that make them useful for decision making. A stratified sample of 250 key mental health decision makers and researchers was drawn from the federal, state, and local levels. Of the 255 eventually interviewed, 155 were mental health decision makers. Of these, 51 were from top federal positions with the Alcohol, Drug Abuse and Mental Health Administration of the Department of Health, Education and Welfare and its institutes (National Institute of Mental Health, National Institute of Alcoholism and Alcohol Abuse, and National Institute of Drug Abuse); 52 were from the highest tier of positions in 10 state departments of mental health; and 52 were local decision makers who administered mental health centers and mental hospitals. The remaining 100 respondents were social science researchers engaged in government-funded mental health research and members of

Alcohol, Drug Abuse and Mental Health Administration research grant review committees.

The task for these 255 people was to review and rate two abstracts from a group of 50 abstracts, based on research reports completed between 1970 and 1974 under sponsorship of the above-named three institutes. These 50 studies were selected to be representative (e.g., in terms of type of study, type and size of sample, ambiguity of results), with purposive variation of three dimensions: the manipulability of the major explanatory variables, the administrative feasibility of the implications, and the degree of congruence with prevailing beliefs in the mental health field. Every abstract was assigned to two occupants of the five different positions in the sample, with an attempt made to match the content of the abstract with the job responsibilities of respondents.

Respondents were interviewed by trained interviewers. During these sessions, respondents rated each of the two abstracts on several measures of usefulness and on 29 descriptive characteristics. The usefulness measures were drawn primarily from answers to two questions: (1) "Assuming your office had to consider the issues discussed in the study, how likely is it that you would take the study results into account?" and (2) "Focusing for a moment just on the study's findings, and not considering external constraints, to what extent does the study contain *ideas or information* that can contribute to the work of your agency?" In addition, respondents indicated whom the most appropriate user of the study would be, then answered the same two usefulness questions for this person. Finally, respondents judged the types of purposes study results would serve. The 29 descriptive characteristics included such items as "Deals with high priority issue," "Contains explicit recommendations," and "Provides quantitative data."

The Knorr Study

The second utilization study (Knorr, 1977) was concerned primarily with an investigation of the extent to which decision makers use research to legitimate decisions or to form decisions. Knorr interviewed 70 medium-level decision makers employed in Austrian federal and municipal government agencies and all directly involved with contract research. These 70 people constituted a "more-or-less complete set of government contractors in the city of Vienna" (1977: 165). The sample consisted only of government officials who recently had funded at least one social science project which was complete at the time of the interview. The studies were in the areas of sociology (51%), economics (24%), educational sciences (13.5%), urban and regional planning (4.5%), political science (4.5%), and other (2.5%).

During the interviews, the government officials were questioned about the social science project (or projects) recently completed. They responded to both open- and closed-ended general questions about how the projects came about, how the results were expected to be utilized, and how the results ultimately were utilized. More specific questions asked were:

> What kind of interest played an essential role in initiating the project and what expectations did those supporting the project have; to what degree were expectations made clear to the researcher, or how specific were the demands made upon the researchers; how could the results of the project in fact be utilized; are there any practical measures that were taken on the basis of the project that would not have been taken otherwise; if yes, what were the effects; and similar questions [Knorr, 1977: 180].

The Patton and Associates Study

The purpose of the utilization study by Patton and his associates (1975: 3) was "to identify and refine a few key variables that may make a major difference in a significant number of evaluation cases." These researchers' method was to follow up 20 federal health evaluations, selected from among a population of 76 evaluations on file in the Office of Health Evaluation, in the Department of Health, Education and Welfare, which were "(1) program evaluation studies of (2) national scope where (3) some systematic data collection was done and (4) where the study was completed no earlier than 1971 and no later than 1973" (1975: 5). The 20 states were drawn randomly from five strata of "nature of program" to assure a representative, heterogeneous sample.

Three key informants were interviewed for each of the 20 studies: the project officer, the most relevant decision maker for the program (identified by the project officer), and the evaluator responsible for the study.

The project officer interviews were conducted primarily to identify decision makers and evaluators. Two interview forms were developed, with some similar questions for the decision makers and the evaluators. Questions were open-ended and covered these areas:

(1) interviewee background, involvement in the program, and involvement in the study
(2) purposes and objectives of the evaluation
(3) political context
(4) expectations during the study about how the findings would be used
(5) major findings from the evaluation
(6) ways in which the study had an impact on program operations, program planning, program policy, and so on
(7) nonprogram impacts, that is, broader impacts on issues associated with the evaluation, position papers, new legislation, and so on
(8) impact and reception of specific study recommendations
(9) factors explaining the study's impact including specific questions on relevant factors taken from the utilization literature on evaluation research
(10) general questions on interviewee's observations about evaluation research and its utilization.

The Alkin and Associates Study

This utilization study (Alkin et al., 1979) aimed at a comprehensive assessment of the course, role, and consequences of evaluation. These evaluation researchers selected five recently completed education evaluation programs (all ESEA Title I or Title-C programs) which they knew of or which were suggested to them. "Approachability of site personnel" and proximity were considerations in selecting the five sites, but the researchers "sought to avoid 'showcase' programs" (p. 36) and to balance the sample with a variety of program types.

The method used to study utilization was a series of interviews with evaluator and program personnel for each case. In these interviews, the researchers made a point of being nondirective, "to allow the interviewees, the 'informants,' to tell the story of the program and its evaluation in their own words, letting each person choose the topics they thought important to discuss" (Alkin et al., 1979: 37). Nonetheless, the researchers were aware of various factors from the evaluation literature (e.g., characteristics of the program staff and evaluator, purposes of the evaluation, quality of the interactions among the participants) and probed for information about these factors on the rare occasions when it was not provided spontaneously.

From these interviews, the researchers assembled a draft report on each evaluation project which attempted to describe and analyze the complete story of the evaluation. These drafts were passed to the interviewees for their comments and reactions, then were revised as needed. The final case studies each contain reactions from the interviewees to the case study which were gleaned from their responses to a loosely structured, open-ended questionnaire.

The Heiss Study

This study (Heiss, 1974) differs from those already presented in that it focused on the use of urban, municipal research. City policy makers and the directors of an innovative urban policy research project (The Urban Observatory) from five U.S. cities were questioned. The cities selected (San Diego, Albuquerque, Denver, Milwaukee, and Boston) were chosen because they were among 10 U.S. cities with Urban Observatories and because the Urban Observatory directors in these cities had been more active with city officials and also agreed to participate. City policy makers included the mayor, city manager, councilmen, aldermen, and city commissioners.

Two questionnaires were developed: one for policy makers and one for observatory directors. These questionnaires, which were mailed to the respondents, generally contained brief, fixed-response questions concerning the extent to which policy makers were exposed to urban policy research, the degree to which they used such research, and the reasons for use or nonuse.

The Urban Institute Study

Like the Heiss study, the study by three researchers from the urban institute (Burt et al., 1972) is an assessment of use of social research by local government decision makers. Ten policy analyses conducted by local governments themselves were selected, with no special attention given to representativeness. Rather, the researchers looked for studies completed during a particular time period (i.e., 1968-1969) and for which there was adequate documentation. The 10 cases analyzed fire boat use (2 cases), fire station location, emergency ambulance service, mechanical street sweeping, on-site incinerations, solid waste collection and disposal, swimming opportunities, subemployment, and venereal disease control.

The procedure was to read all documentation, then interview the major study participants and the intended users. Based on this information, the researchers made ratings of the impact (or utility) of each policy analyst and the reasons for the impact, focusing on 13 different factors (e.g., city size, study timing, decision-maker interest, proposed changes).

The Caplan and Associates Study

In this study (Caplan et al., 1975; Caplan, 1977), federal-level officials were interviewed regarding their use of empirically based social science knowledge (exclusive of "orthodox economic research") in policy-related decision making. These researchers interviewed 204 officials "holding important positions across the various departments and major agencies and commissions of the executive branch of the United States government" (Caplan, 1977: 184). Of the 204 respondents, 15% were at the secretary level (i.e., undersecretary, deputy undersecretary, assistant undersecretary, or assistant secretary); 27% were directors of institutes, commissioners, or other governmental units; 33% were deputy or assistant directors, upper-level administrators, and bureau or division chiefs; and 25% were "agency personnel . . . of somewhat lesser authority" (Caplan, 1977: 184).

Interviews of about one and a half hours were conducted with each of these officials. Using a standard list of questions, the interviewers asked each official to identify instances of social science knowledge use which had affected policy decisions. Responses were written and tape recorded for later analysis.

The Rich Study

Rich (1977) conducted a case study of the Continuous National Survey, a project funded by the National Science Foundation and executed by the National Opinion Research Center. This project was to provide policy makers from federal domestic service-oriented agencies with policy-relevant public opinion data on a continuous basis. Thirteen different national surveys were conducted over the twelve-month project period using questions developed by the federal agency participants. Rich interviewed survey clients from seven federal agencies. "In-depth interviews" were conducted with 38 respondents at each of five different times during the Continuous National Survey. These respondents were all agency participants involved with the administration on utilization of the survey results, the National Opinion Research Center project staff, and the National Science Foundation grant administrators for the survey. All 38 respondents were interviewed one final time about nine months after the end of the survey.

These interviews appear to have involved loosely structured questions about the type and extent of utilization of the information from the survey waves. It should be noted that the information on the methodology of this study was limited; consequently, the description and analysis of this study in the next section are tentative and less definitive than in the other seven cases.

ANALYSIS OF THE STUDIES

These studies can be compared on a number of methodological dimensions. The six dimensions of analysis considered here were selected because they reflect important components of any type of judgment: what is judged (basis, time frame, definition and comprehensiveness of dimensions), who makes the judgments (subjects), and how are the judgments made (measurement method). Figure 1 contains comparative data on six methodological aspects of the studies. Each of these aspects will be defined and described below.

Basis of Judgment

In seven of the eight studies, the judgments of utility made by respondents were based on actual projects. That is, these research projects either

FIGURE 1: Utilization Studies Characterized on Seven Methodological Aspects

ASPECTS STUDY	Basis for Judgments	Time Orientation of Judgments	Subjects	Measurement Method	Definition of Use	Focus of Study Primary	Focus of Study Secondary
Weiss and Bucuvalas	Similar projects	Future	Mental health decisionmakers (federal, state and local levels); researchers	Interviews; rating of usefulness by subjects	Broad: conceptual and/or instrumental	Outcome	Process
Knorr	Actual projects	Past	Government officials (Austria); federal & local levels	Interviews; coding of responses	Broad: symbolic, conceptual, instrumental	Outcome	Goals Processes
Patton et al	Actual projects	Past	Federal health agency project officers, decisionmakers and evaluators	Interviews; coding of responses	Broad: conceptual instrumental	Outcome	Goals Processes
Alkin et al	Actual projects	Past	Local Project personnel and evaluators	Interviews; collation of responses	Broad: conceptual, instrumental	Outcome	Goals Inputs Processes
Heiss	Actual projects	Past	City policymakers; policy research unit directors	Questionnaire; fixed responses	Broad: conceptual instrumental	Outcome	Process
Urban Institute	Actual projects	Past	Local Policymakers and policy analysts	Interviews; coding of responses	Broad but oriented toward instrumental	Outcome	Process
Caplan et al.	Actual projects	Past	Federal executive-level decisionmakers	Interviews; coding of responses	Broad: conceptual, instrumental	Outcome	Inputs Process
Rich	Actual projects	Present	Federal officials of domestic service agencies	Interviews; coding of responses	Broad: conceptual, instrumental	Outcome	Goals Inputs Process

were in progress at the time of the judgments or, more commonly, were completed at the time of the judgments. In both cases, however, the basis for judgments was actual projects of the agency, department, or unit in which the subject was located. Because these projects were being or had been conducted by the subjects' unit, the subject based his or her judgments of utilization on the actual utilization experiences of the unit on these particular projects.

The Weiss and Bucuvalas study involved a different basis for utilization judgments. Subjects rated actual studies, but these studies had not necessarily been conducted by their unit. The studies, however, were similar to those undertaken by the subjects' unit. Unlike the other seven studies, then, the Weiss and Bucuvalas study generally involved subjects' judgments of hypothetical use rather than judgments of actual use.

Time Orientation of Judgments

In six of the eight cases, respondents were asked to make judgments about projects which already were completed; consequently, the time orientation of their judgments was to the past. In another study, the Weiss and Bucuvalas study, the judgments were about likely future usage in the event that the study had been real. In the Rich study, the judgments had a "present" time orientation; that is, judgments were provided while the utilization process was occurring.

Subjects

A variety of respondents was used, from decision makers to project personnel and researchers. In half of the studies (i.e., Weiss and Bucuvalas, Patton et al., Atkin et al., and Heiss), at least two different general types of subjects were used (e.g., decision makers and evaluators). In the other studies, only one general type of subject was used, although the level of the subjects sometimes varied (e.g., in the Knorr study, both federal- and local-level government officials served as subjects). In all cases, those most directly involved in research utilization served as respondents.

Measurement Method

Interviews were employed in seven cases, and questionnaires were used in the eighth, the Heiss study. In general, respondents gave answers to open-ended questions, which the researchers then coded. Only in the Weiss and Bucuvalas study did respondents make quantitative ratings of usefulness and of the factors related to it.

Definition of Use

In all of the studies, the researchers defined use broadly. Utilization can be defined in terms of two primary types of use: instrumental or conceptual (Pelz, 1978; Rich, 1977). Instrumental use involves changes in practices and procedures which are a direct result of evaluation findings. Conceptual use involves general changes in a policy maker's or a program director's viewpoint on policies or programs related to an evaluation study. A related type of usage, symbolic, also can occur. Symbolic use refers to the underlying rationale for using evaluation findings, whether instrumental or conceptual.

In the eight studies considered here, both instrumental and conceptual (and occasionally symbolic) usage were counted. Perhaps for this reason, the large majority of these studies concluded that usage generally was high.

Focus of Study

This aspect refers to the comprehensiveness of the evaluation studies, that is, the extent to which four main foci of general evaluation studies are considered. These foci are program (1) goals, (2) inputs, (3) processes, and (4) outcomes (see Conner, 1980, for a more detailed discussion). In the "Primary" Focus of Study column of Figure 1, the most relevant component is listed, with the component(s) of secondary importance listed in the next column. All of the studies focused primarily on outcome. Process was a secondary interest of all of the studies, but process has an unusual definition here, considering the retrospective or prospective orientation of most of the studies. In the evaluation research model, process refers to the dynamic of the study and is assessed while it occurs. In six of the studies reported here, the dynamic had passed, and the respondents were making static post hoc assessments of the process. In the Weiss and Bucuvalas study, one dynamic process is tapped (i.e., that of the respondent making utilization judgments) but another important dynamic process—that of the unit's discussion of and decision on usage—is missed. In the Rich study, the dynamic process was tapped while it was occurring and at several points in the utilization process.

CRITIQUE OF THE STUDIES AND DISCUSSION

The categorization of the eight studies on these methodological dimensions reveals several interesting aspects of the focus and approach of these particular utilization studies. These studies are notable in their primary focus on actual evaluation projects as the basis for subject judgments. The primary advantage of this focus is the clear link to actual instances of utilization. Another advantage is that these judgments are intended to be objective reports of what occurred or was occurring rather than subjective guesses of what might occur. One disadvantage of this type of focus, particularly in retrospective studies, is the post hoc quality of the judgments. Can we be sure that the reports of utilization are valid? How confident can we be that the subjects' reports have not been biased by the events which have intervened between the utilization decisions and the time of judgment? A further disadvantage, from a scientific viewpoint, is the inability of the evaluation researcher to intervene to some extent in the process to test the effects of important variables.

The Weiss and Bucuvalas study demonstrates how similar rather than actual studies can be used to permit some intervention by the evaluation researcher. These researchers gave subjects two research report abstracts from a group of 50 such abstracts. These 50 abstracts were based on studies selected with purposive variation on three dimensions: the manipulability of the major explanatory variables, the administrative feasibility of the implications, and the degree of congruence with prevailing beliefs in the mental health field. The multiple regression approach used by Weiss and Bucuvalas permitted some assessment of the importance of these dimensions. This "similar projects" approach for the basis of judgments in utilization studies has great potential because of the possibility that experimental tests of theoretically important utilization dimensions could be undertaken.

Another noteworthy aspect of these eight studies is the general orientation on judgments of past utilization. Only two studies had either a future or present time orientation for subjects' judgments. The absence of more studies with a present or current time orientation is a serious missing link in the utilization research chain. We have, it would appear, a sufficient number of studies with a retrospective orientation to formulate several good models of evaluation utilization and to identify the important factors of these models. These models, then, could be used to guide a utilization researcher in a study of the dissemination and utilization of research *while it is occurring.* Although difficult to implement, this type of study is essential if we are to obtain the most accurate information about utilization. Retrospective studies, while useful, are subject to biases directly related to the type of use which has occurred. Likewise, "future" time orientation studies are subject to biases related to what judges think or hope will occur, not necessarily what actually will occur. The Rich study employed a "present" time orientation; this resulted in new insights about the utilization process. More studies of this type would be useful.

The subjects for these eight studies generally included the decision makers for whom the studies would be most relevant. In half of the studies, the subjects also included other types of relevant participants (e.g., agency evaluators or policy analysts). The inclusion of two or more participants from the same agency or department is a good practice since this permits some analysis of consistency of judgments across individuals assessing the same project.

The results of these eight studies would have been even more convincing if the list of subjects had been expanded to include those slightly higher in the hierarchy than the decision makers who typically were included. The inclusion of decision makers at a variety of levels would permit comparisons among the levels in degree and type of utilization. It may be, for example, that different factors affect the type and degree of utilization within a department or unit than affect utilization at an agency level (i.e., across several units or departments). Likewise, utilization factors may differ for local- or state-level decision makers, compared with federal-level decision makers. The Caplan et al. study, for instance, uncovered different types of decision-maker styles at the federal, executive level; these may apply for decision makers at other levels. These comments on study subjects suggest that one useful approach for further utilization studies may be to hold the basis of judgment constant (e.g., "similar" studies of educational projects) while investigating any differences in the utilization judgments of decision makers and evaluators at the local, state, and federal levels.

In regard to measurement methods, these utilization studies have relied too heavily on the use of open-ended interviews and questionnaires. Although this is understandable (in view of the retrospective orientation of most of the studies), enough utilization factors now have been identified to permit more systematic quantitative assessments by respondents. The Weiss and Bucuvalas study is noteworthy in this regard for its use of rating scales.

One important element missing from this group of evaluation studies is data on reliability of judgments. Whether subjects make ratings or interviewees' open-ended questionnaire answers are coded, the utilization scores which result from these methods should be checked for their reliability.

More studies using more quantitative methods will not be sufficient to provide new insights in the utilization process. In addition, more qualitative studies need to be done which use naturalistic research methods to capture the utilization process as it occurs. Alkin and his associates attempted to do this in their retrospective study of local educational evaluations. Their qualitative study revealed interesting dynamics in the course of evaluation implementation and utilization.

Finally, two components of general evaluation approaches have not received enough attention: goals and inputs. Again, this probably is a function of the retrospective focus of most of these studies; in this case, goals and inputs other than the most obvious ones are difficult to identify. As more studies are conducted of dissemination utilization efforts while they are occurring, we will be able to identify the multiple goals and varied inputs which are part of the utilization process. The Rich study, with its "present" time focus, and the Alkin et al. study, with its retrospective time focus but detailed and qualitative approach, are unusual in that each uncovered more detailed information than usual about goals and inputs.

These eight utilization studies, while they have some shortcomings, demonstrate the utility to evaluation research of studying the utilization process closely. These studies have uncovered important factors affecting utilization which can help to guide future utilization studies so that their results will be more likely to be used. This review and analysis has identified several gaps in the focus of past utilization studies and has suggested some new approaches. Future studies of utilization may be able to implement these new approaches and increase our understanding of the utilization process.

REFERENCES

ALKIN, M. D., R. DAILLAK, and P. WHITE (1979) Using Evaluations: Does Evaluation Make a Difference? Beverly Hills, CA: Sage.

ARGYRIS, C. (1965) Organization and Innovation. Homewood, IL: Dorsey Press.

BECK, M. A. (1978) "Effecting the research to action linkage: The Research Utilization Program of NILECJ." Washington, DC: National Institute of Law Enforcement and Criminal Justice, Law Enforcement Assistance Administration.

BENNIS, W. G., K. D. BENNE, R. CHIN, and K. E. COREY [eds.] (1976) The Planning of Change. New York: Holt, Rinehart and Winston.

BERNSTEIN, I. and H. E. FREEMAN (1975) Academic and Entrepreneurial Research: Consequences of Diversity in Federal Evaluation Studies. New York: Russell Sage.

BURT, M. R., D. M. FISK, and H. P. HATRY (1972) Factors affecting the impact of urban policy analysis: Ten case histories (Working Paper 201-3). Washington, DC: Urban Institute.

CAPLAN, N. (1977) "A minimal set of conditions necessary for the utilization of social science knowledge in policy formulation at the national level," pp. 183-197 in C. H. Weiss (ed.) Using Social Research in Public Policy Making. Lexington, MA: D. C. Heath.

——— A. MORRISON, and R. J. STAMBAUGH (1975) The use of social science knowledge in policy decisions at the national level. Ann Arbor: University of Michigan, Center for Research on Utilization of Scientific Knowledge.

CHESTER, M. and M. FLANDERS (1967) "Resistance to research and research utilization: The death and life of a feedback attempt." Journal of Applied Behavioral Science 3: 469-487.

COE, R. M. and E. A. BERNHILL (1967) "Social dimensions of failure in innovation." Human Organization 26: 149-156.

CONNER, R. F. (1980) "The evaluation of research utilization," in M. Klein and K. Teilmann (eds.) Handbook of Criminal Justice Evaluation. Beverly Hills, CA: Sage.

DAVIS, H. E. and S. SALASIN (1975) "The utilization of evaluation," pp. 621-666 in E. L. Struening and M. Guttentag (eds.) Handbook of Evaluation Research (Vol. 1). Beverly Hills, CA: Sage.

DEITCHMAN, S. (1976) The Best-Laid Schemes: A Tale of Social Research and Bureaucracy. Cambridge: MIT Press.

EMRICK, J. A. and S. M. PETERSON (1978) A Synthesis of Findings Across Five Recent Studies in Educational Dissemination and Change. San Francisco: Far West Laboratory.

FAIRWEATHER, G. W. (1967) Methods for Experimental Social Innovation. New York: John Wiley.

———— D. H. SANDERS and L. G. TORNATZKY (1974) Creating Change in Mental Health Organizations. New York: Pergamon.

GEIS, G. (1975) "Program descriptions in criminal justice evaluations," pp. 87-96 in E. Viano (ed.) Criminal Justice Research. Lexington, MA: D. C. Heath.

GLASER, E. M. and S. TAYLOR (1973) "Factors influencing the success of applied research." American Psychologist 28: 140-146.

GOODWIN, L. (1975) Can Social Science Help Resolve National Problems? New York: Free Press.

HARGROVE, E. C. (1975) The Missing Link: The Study of the Implementation of Social Policy. Washington, DC: Urban Institute.

HAVELOCK, R. G. (1976) "Research on utilization of knowledge," in M. Kochen (ed.) Information for Action: Reorganizing Knowledge for Wisdom. New York: Academic Press.

———— (1969) Planning for innovation through dissemination and utilization of knowledge. Ann Arbor: University of Michigan, Center for Research on Utilization of Scientific Knowledge.

HEISS, R. W. (1974) Urban research and urban policymaking: An observatory perspective. Boulder: University of Colorado, Bureau of Governmental Research and Service.

Human Interaction Research Institute and National Institute of Mental Health (1976) Putting knowledge to use: A distillation of the literature regarding knowledge transfer and change. Los Angeles: Author.

KNORR, K. D. (1977) "Policymakers' use of social science knowledge: Symbolic or instrumental?" pp. 165-182 in C. H. Weiss (ed.) Using Social Research in Public Policy Making. Lexington, MA: D. C. Heath.

National Academy of Sciences (1968) The Behavioral Sciences and the Federal Government. Washington, DC: Government Printing Office.

PATTON, M. Q., P. S. GRIMES, K. M. GUTHRIE, N. J. BRENNAN, B. D. FRENCH, and D. A. BLYTH (1975) "In search of impact: An analysis of the utilization of federal health evaluation research." Minneapolis: University of Minnesota, Minnesota Center for Social Research. [Slightly abridged version, pp. 141-163 in Weiss, 1977.]

PELZ, D. C. (1978) "Some expanded perspectives on use of social science in public policy," pp. 346-359 in J. M. Yinger and S. J. Cutler (eds.) Major Social Issues: A Multidisciplinary View. New York: Free Press.

RICH, R. F. (1977) "Uses of social science information by federal bureaucrats: Knowledge for action versus knowledge for understanding," pp. 199-211 in C. H. Weiss (ed.) Using Social Research in Public Policy Making. Lexington, MA: D. C. Heath.

Social Science Research Council (1969) The Behavioral and Social Sciences: Outlook and Need. Englewood Cliffs, NJ: Prentice-Hall.

Special Commission on the Social Sciences, National Science Foundation (1968) Knowledge into Action: Improving the Nation's Use of the Social Sciences. Washington, DC: Government Printing Office.

U.S. House of Representatives, Committee on Governmental Operations (1967) The Use of Social Research in Federal Domestic Programs. Washington, DC: Government Printing Office.

WEEKS, E. C. (1979) "Factors affecting the utilization of evaluation findings in administrative decision-making." Ph.D. dissertation, University of California, Irvine.

WEISS, C. H. [ed.] (1977) Using Social Research in Public Policy Making. Lexington, MA: D. C. Heath.

——— (1972) "Evaluating educational and social action programs: A treeful of owls," pp. 3-27 in C. H. Weiss (ed.) Evaluating Action Programs. Boston: Allyn and Bacon.

——— and M. J. BUCUVALAS (forthcoming) Social Science Research and Decision Making. New York: Columbia University Press.

——— (1977) "The challenge of social research to decision making," pp. 213-233 in C. H. Weiss (ed.) Using Social Research in Public Policy Making. Lexington, MA: D. C. Heath.

WHOLEY, J. S., J. W. SCANLON, H. G. DUFFY, J. S. FIKUMOTO, and L. M. VOGT (1971) Federal Evaluation Policy. Washington, DC: Urban Institute.

4

MEASURING UTILIZATION OF MENTAL HEALTH PROGRAM CONSULTATION

Judith K. Larsen
Paul D. Werner

*American Institutes for Research in the
Behavioral Sciences
Palo Alto, California*

The problem of measurement is one of the most crucial issues in the study of information utilization. Its importance has become increasingly evident in an ongoing program of investigation at American Institutes for Research studying program-oriented consultation to community mental health centers. This research concerned dissemination of information by program consultants to center administrators and staff. One approach to assessing the impact of such consultations focused on utilization of consultants' suggestions by the center. The methodological issues raised in our analyses highlight the necessity of measuring alternative types of information utilization and of applying multiple strategies for assessing its correlates.

ALTERNATIVE TYPES OF UTILIZATION

Introduction

Basic to the assessment and study of information utilization is the assumption that we know what we are attempting to measure—that we

AUTHORS' NOTE: We would like to acknowledge the contributions of Eleanor L. Norris and Angeline M. Jacobs in conceptualizing the issues discussed in this chapter.

know what information utilization is. At the least, there must be some common agreement of what information utilization is in each particular instance, or general acceptance of a set of alternative and specific definitions.

Because of the complex nature of utilization, it has been difficult to arrive at one definition which is both precise and comprehensive. In fact, the question of what constitutes utilization is one of the most salient issues in the field. It is now generally recognized that there are many ways in which information can be utilized. Utilization has facets entailing different behaviors on the part of the information recipient and information source. In the early days of utilization research, however, this complexity was not generally acknowledged. For example, early research tended to define utilization as implementation of an entire set of recommendations in the form suggested by the researcher. One reason for this assumption was that the pioneering studies were conducted by rural sociologists investigating the diffusion of agricultural innovations like hybrid corn seed (Ryan and Gross, 1943). For the farmers under study, the complete adoption of improved seed was almost universally advantageous. Since it was biologically impossible to modify hybrid corn seeds, it was commonly accepted that utilization meant complete adoption. This all-or-none definition of utilization entered the basic research paradigm and was adopted in countless subsequent studies of knowledge implementation.

Yet, for better or worse, agricultural innovations are not the same as social program changes. Information relevant to social programs, unlike hybrid corn seeds, can be modified, can be only partially used, can be used in alternative ways, or can justifiably not be used at all. Initially, researchers did not detect these differences because they were closely following the all-or-none approach. More recent scrutiny of the utilization process has suggested that complete adoption—in which the user implements the information in the exact form in which it was suggested—is not the only form of utilization. In fact, it may be the exception. There are many circumstances in which complete adoption would be inappropriate.

Categories of Utilization and Nonutilization

More recently, researchers have acknowledged alternative forms of utilization and have attempted to incorporate these into their studies.

Seven alternative forms of utilization—and nonutilization—were used in our research with community mental health centers. There were four types of utilization and three types of nonutilization.

UTILIZATION

Complete implementation as presented. The first, implementation of information presented, has already been discussed. It is complete adoption of information in the form originally presented.

Adaptation of information. In some settings it is not possible to implement information in its original form, but the information may work well if changed somewhat to meet the circumstances of the user. In these cases, a considerable degree of adaptation or modification may take place in the utilization process. Users may adapt the information to fit their own needs, or there may be mutual adaptation between the user and the producer (e.g., Campeau et al., 1978; Berman and McLaughlin, 1977).

Partial use of information. Especially when the information consists of more than a simple fact, the user may find that some aspects of the information are more relevant and applicable than others. The user may select and use those portions which are appropriate and discard or disregard the others.

Steps have been taken toward implementation although full implementation has not yet occurred. For much information, a period of preparation or anticipation is required before adoption can be accomplished. During this stage, the preliminaries of adoption are worked out, administrative and organizational obstacles are identified, and plans made for addressing them. This form of utilization may be seen as a volatile one. Because preparation for implementation has begun, there is a high likelihood that adoption will follow, but there is also the possibility that the obstacles uncovered will prevent utilization from being achieved.

These four categories of utilization seem to have particular relevance to the study of information diffusion in applied contexts such as those involving social science information. However, they do not exhaust the range of possible outcomes of presentation of information, because they omit outcomes in which nonutilization occurred. As Weiss (1977) notes, there is an inherent belief among many utilization researchers that adoption *should* result from the presentation of information. In other words, utilization is thought of as desirable; its opposite, nonutilization, is seen as undesirable and even unfortunate. Because nonutilization has been viewed as something to be avoided or corrected, historically there has been little detailed and systematic study of aspects of nonutilization. The present study, however, examined three types of nonutilization of information.

NONUTILIZATION

Information has been considered by a potential user but then rejected. In this case one or more decision makers have devoted time and effort to studying the information, and a decision has been made against implementation. Nonutilization in this case occurs after the information has been given a hearing, whereas nonutilization, categorized as "nothing done," involves rejection without clear consideration.

Nothing is done with the information. This type of nonutilization includes those cases in which no action and not even discussion of the information has occurred. The information is, essentially, ignored without further thought.

Implementation of the information has not occurred, but it is under consideration. In this case, no action has been taken, however, discussion and deliberation about the information have occurred. Consideration of the information may be somewhat abstract, although fact-finding about the implications of adoption and nonadoption may also occur.

Development of the Categories

Since it is commonly acknowledged that information utilization is difficult to measure accurately, considerable effort was devoted to the development of the categories. An early step was a review of the literature for examples of previous empirical research. At the time of the review, there were only a handful of such studies, and none that we could locate dealing with information utilization in local human service organizations such as community mental health centers. Therefore, more theoretical literature was used to identify issues likely to be critical in our research. For the most part, this included identification of different conceptualizations of utilization. Those that appeared to be comparable, even though called by different names, were grouped together. This approach provided a theoretical indication of the types of utilization possibilities that we could expect in our study.

Prior to the current study, we conducted pilot studies in which much of the development of utilization alternatives was accomplished. The basic research methodology employed was that of training an observer to note information provided to a user organization by a consultant. Data on the dependent variable, information utilization, were collected by means of a follow-up interview of potential users. The interviews involved open-ended inquiries about the status of each idea presented by the consultant, the purpose being to determine whether the information was used, why or why not, and in what way it had been implemented or not implemented. These open-ended responses were then inductively classified into general categories. Project staff who conducted the classification were familiar with the results of the literature review and therefore were alerted to the types of utilization possibilities thought to be present. The result of this process was identification of the types or classes of utilization discussed in the previous section.

MEASUREMENT OF UTILIZATION

Scaling Issues

The seven types of utilization and nonutilization described previously are enumerated in Figure 1. For the purposes of the research to be reported, they have been listed roughly in order of the degree of utilization judged to be entailed in each. That is, "Considered and rejected" is viewed as entailing the least utilization (or, in other words, the most nonutilization), whereas "Implemented and adapted to fit user's needs" is viewed as involving the highest level of utilization of the currently described categories. The number preceding each category may be taken as its value in an ordinal scale.

The assumption that we have made, that these utilization categories approximate at least an ordinal scale, warrants further discussion. When a characteristic is measured at the ordinal level, differences in the size of numerical scale values reflect differences in the magnitude of the underlying characteristic. In our list of utilization and nonutilization categories, a

FIGURE 1: Utilization and Non-Utilization Categories
and Their Definitions

1. Considered and rejected. Some discussion took place, but the finding is no longer being considered.
2. Nothing done. No action, not even discussion, was taken.
3. Under consideration. The information had not been used, however it was being considered and discussed.
4. Steps taken toward implementation. Although the information had not been used, the decision to do so had been made and steps toward it had been taken.
5. Partially implemented. Certain features of the information had been used while others had been disregarded.
6. Implemented as presented. The information had not been used in the past, and was used in its original form.
7. Implemented and adapted to fit user's needs. The information had not been used in the past. Certain features of the finding were modified or adpated to fit the local situation.

6 is assumed to reflect more utilization than a 5, a 5 more than a 4, and so on. This approach to ordering the categories was developed on the basis of careful consideration of the degree of utilization represented in each category. Yet it is acknowledged that there will not be total consensus. We are currently developing methods of assessing the validity of the proposed ordering. For the present, though, the ordering that has been described should be viewed as a working assumption that provides the basis for preliminary analyses, but that is also subject to modification.

An alternative interpretation of the categorization is that it is a nominal scale, in which the numerical values are merely names for the categories. In this case, the numbers in Figure 1 could just as easily be randomly chosen letters. If the listing in Figure 1 is viewed as reflecting the nominal level of measurement, then a score of 6 indicates a different amount of utilization from a score of 5, but not necessarily more or less utilization. It is clear that the 7 categories are, for the most part, distinct, and we feel some degree of order is involved. The assumption that the categories can be rank-ordered allows application of more sensitive and statistically powerful quantitative methods than could be utilized if assessment at only the nominal level is assumed.

Another level of measurement that may apply to the categories in Figure 1 is the interval level. If utilization is measured at this level, the numerical scale values reflect not only ordering but also specifiable differences in "true" utilization level. That is, an idea utilized at level 6 would entail as much more utilization over an idea utilized at level 5 as an idea at level 5 does over an idea utilized at level 4. While our utilization categories clearly do not form a true interval scale, a case may be made for the scale's having interval properties at some score levels. In this case, this measure may be akin to many employed by social scientists in being somewhere between the ordinal and the interval level. Assuming that utilization is being measured at the interval level permits use of statistics involving summing of scale values as well as multiplication and division. For example, it is not appropriate to calculate the mean utilization of a set of innovations unless it can be assumed that utilization forms an interval scale.

The Two Levels of Study of the Correlates of Utilization

The correlates of information utilization may be studied from two perspectives: first, at the level of the individual suggestion and, next, at the level of all suggestions given in the process of information exchange. As adoption of this two-level analytic strategy has important methodological implications, its rationale will be discussed in some detail. The basis for this two-level approach is the fact that in most cases of information utilization, more than one suggestion or idea is given to the prospective user. As a result, different data bear on the utilization of individual ideas as opposed to utilization of the set of ideas presented.

UTILIZATION OF INDIVIDUAL IDEAS

One level of study of utilization is to ask what led to utilization or nonutilization of each particular suggestion. Here analysis is at the level of correlates of utilization of the individual suggestion. Primary concern at this level cannot be on the general characteristics of the information-giving transaction (e.g., the characteristics of the information giver or the user), because these characteristics are constant for all ideas given during the transaction. To illustrate, a particular consultant to a community mental health center in our study made 20 suggestions to center staff. It was found upon follow-up questioning of the staff that 1 of these suggestions had been considered and rejected, that nothing had been done about 2, that steps had been taken to implement 4, that 3 had been partially implemented, that 4 had been implemented as presented, and that 6 had been adapted. In this case it would be impossible to distinguish among ideas utilized at different levels (e.g., those in category 2 versus those in category 6) on the basis of consultant characteristics or characteristics of the organization. The reason that such a distinction could not be made is that the set of consultant and organizational characteristics impacting on implementation for each of these ideas was identical. Each of these 20 ideas had been presented by the same information giver to the same organization. Thus, in this case, study of general characteristics such as the consultant's level of supportiveness or the organization's degree of preparation would be uninformative.

Experience has suggested that it would be more appropriate, as a method of studying correlates of individual utilization scores, to concentrate on the particular characteristics of each suggestion. Suggestions may be differentiated from one another on the basis of characteristics such as their cost and complexity, that is, some are costly to implement and others are inexpensive to implement. As differences on these dimensions can be observed among ideas within a single information exchange transaction, these may be appropriately studied as correlates of ideas' varying levels of utilization.

OVERALL UTILIZATION OF A SET OF IDEAS

For study of overall level of utilization, there is little problem in choosing variables to be studied as correlates. These would include variables that characterize the situation studied in toto, such as the style of the information-giver and the user's readiness for change.

On the other hand, the choice of a method for summarizing overall utilization is a difficult one. This problem arises because it does not seem appropriate to assume that the utilization categories listed in Figure 1 form an interval scale. As a result, utilization in an information exchange cannot be summarized by computing the mean utilization category of the information given. Summary statistics appropriate for ordinal level data, such as the median and mode, also seem inappropriate because they do not incorporate much information about outcomes in each particular utilization category.

One approach to deriving summary scores is to simply count the number of ideas that are classified in each utilization category for each situation studied. This procedure has the disadvantage of yielding results that are strongly influenced by the total number of suggestions given. For example, to find that 6 suggestions were fully implemented has very different implications if only 6 suggestions were made than if 30 suggestions were made. To correct for number of suggestions, we chose to compute the *percentage* of ideas in each utilization category for each case.

Combination of Categories and Formation of New Scales

The utilization categories discussed above do not have to be treated as separate categories; they can be combined in any number of ways to facilitate the measurement problem at hand. For example, if the purpose of the research is to identify a range of utilization alternatives, it would be most appropriate to use a broad number of categories to capitalize on the distinctions among types of utilization and nonutilization. However, if the purpose of the research is to determine general classes of utilization, large numbers of categories could produce more information than the researcher wants or needs. Therefore, there may be many cases in which combining the seven categories into fewer more inclusive categories is preferred.

The current study decided to try this approach and developed a three-category classification. The categories are:

(1) no utilization (considered and rejected; nothing done)
(2) interest in idea (under consideration; steps being taken; partially implemented)
(3) utilization (implemented as presented; adapted to fit user's needs).

The utilization results for ideas can be classified into these three categories; similarly the percentage of ideas in each category can be computed for any case.

As mentioned above, we found it desirable to have a single score summarizing the utilization of a set of idea. Our overall utilization measure included categories clearly indicating utilization and nonutilization. More specifically, the proportion of ideas clearly utilized was determined for each case, and then the proportion of ideas *not* utilized was subtracted to produce an overall indication of outcome. The formula for the measure is the following:

Overall utilization = Utilization percent ⁻ Nonutilization percent + 75.
The constant of 75 was added to avoid negative values.

ANALYSES OF UTILIZATION MEASURES

Research Method

Determining the extent of utilization within these multiple approaches to measurement has been a major issue in our research on utilization of information in community mental health centers. The research, conducted in collaboration with National Institute of Mental Health, includes the study of methods of information dissemination and utilization in community mental health centers throughout the country. One component of the project involved program-oriented consultation. Consultations were arranged by asking a community mental health center to indicate an aspect of its general program which it would like to revise or review, such as children's services, in-patient services, or the like. A consultant recommended by the National Council of Community Mental Health Centers as an expert in the content area and an experienced observer then were matched to the center. The consultant visited the center for a two-day consultation session. Data from 39 such consultations are described below.

Each consultant was accompanied by a trained observer who had the responsibility for collecting data on the consultation. One of the activities of the observer was to collect data on specific suggestions or ideas provided by the consultant. To do this, the observer kept a careful record of each recommendation or suggestion made by the consultant. At the end of the first day of consultation, or at a pause during the second day, the observer and consultant reviewed the list of suggestions. This allowed the consultant to approve the list and to suggest rewording of some ideas to insure they represented the original intent. The exact manner in which the lists of suggestions were used varied among consultations. Some consultants used the list as the basis for a feedback session and reviewed each point with staff, others used the list in a less structured way, and some consultants barely referred to it. In addition to the consultant's copy of the list of ideas, at least two copies were given to staff (more were prepared if a photocopy machine was available), and the observer kept a copy.

At two points in time, four and eight months following the original consultation visit, these lists were used as the basis of follow-up interviews with center staff. The primary purpose of each interview was to learn what, if anything, had been done with each idea—in other words, to determine the nature and extent of utilization. In the present report, data from the four-month follow-up are used. It should be noted that unlike many studies which examine theoretical utilization of research findings or use of products, this research concerns implementation of suggested courses of action—recommendations made by the consultants to the community mental health centers under study.

Data Collected

The techniques we have developed to provide an indication of outcome involve measurement of the multiple components of utilization outlined above.

STATUS

The first component corresponds to the 7-category classification of utilization and nonutilization presented in Figure 1. For the purposes of this presentation, this component is called Status. This was scored for each individual idea, and summary percentage measures covering all of the ideas at a consultation were computed as well. Examples of ideas given by consultants and the utilization status of each at the time of the follow-up interview are presented in Figure 2.

CHARACTERISTICS OF THE INFORMATION

In the current report, five additional aspects of information are considered. They are summarized by the name *Difficulty* and take into account a general estimate of the "quality" of the information. These variables attempt to distinguish information which demands considerable planning and effort from that requiring more minor efforts. Difficulty is conceptualized as including a number of characteristics: (1) number of people required to implement, (2) cost of implementing, (3) time (in terms

FIGURE 2: Examples of Ideas Given by Consultants
and Their Utilization Status

1. Work out a system between the state hospital and the center in which the client discharged from the hospital has more than a three-day supply of medicine. It has been shown that a high proportion of readmissions are the result of clients having problems with medications when they leave the hospital. Therefore, try to see that the clients have more than a three day's supply of medication upon discharge, or enable the client to receive a prescription from the center prior to discharge.
   —Implemented as presented.
2. Consider the formation of therapy groups in the partial hospitalization program. If initiation of therapy groups has been a problem at the center, the day treatment program may be a forum for starting them. Cohorts or groups of clients, to some degree, are likely to enter the program and be discharged as contemporaries, thus spawning outpatient groups.
   —Under consideration.
3. There are a number of materials already available that would be appropriate for your children's services. For example, consider using the Interpersonal Cognitive Problem Solving series with children rather than developing new materials at the center that would duplicate those already available.
   —Considered and rejected.
4. Negotiate provider status contracts with third-party-payors not currently used, but who are able to reimburse for these kinds of services. This will provide resources for your service program, and will begin building additional revenue sources. (The consultant provided a suggestion of a specific third-party payor, and provided the center with third-party payor information sheets.)
   —Partially implemented.
5. It is important to be concerned with continuity of care, especially when clients are referred to you for some specific service. You have several clients referred by the school. In the case of these children, you could schedule staffings with school counselors, and discuss the cases directly. The staffings could be conducted at the school if that would help.
   —Nothing done.
6. A good deal of new information regarding C&E services is available. Things have been changing, and it would be good if the staff of all services in the center knew about it, not only the C&E staff. Therefore conduct some staff development activities around C&E, including problems of fee collection for such services.
   —Implemented and adapted to fit user's needs.

of person-hours) needed to implement, (4) trialability (in terms of level of difficulty in trying out) the innovation, and (5) complexity (difficulty in understanding the innovation). Each of these was scored on a 3-point scale with 1 indicating low difficulty and 3 indicating high difficulty. Overall difficulty of each idea was computed as the sum of these five scores and could range from 5 to 15. Because difficulty scores of 12 and above occurred rarely, they were merged into category 12, which thus represents ideas that were most troublesome to implement.

Some of the difficulty inherent in implementing a suggestion depends on the capabilities and level of flexibility of the organization to which it is presented. In an organization with a large staff, an innovation requiring the time of 1 full-time staff member may not be burdensome, whereas in an organization having only 10 staff members, the same innovation might be quite difficult to implement. Similarly, the relative impact of cost depends on the organizational context, as does the impact of the other three components of difficulty. This interaction between difficulty and organizational characteristics will not be analyzed in the present report—difficulty will be treated only as a characteristic of each suggestion.

CHARACTERISTICS OF THE CONSULTATION

A large number of measures were developed to assess characteristics of the consultation. These included measures of the consultant's characteristics and style, the organization's characteristics, and factors in the organization's external environment that might affect consultation outcome. To demonstrate the method of studying utilization over all ideas in a consultation, preliminary results are reported for two consultant characteristics: the consultant's encouragement of staff participation and extent of knowledge about the topic of the consultation. These variables were rated by the trained observer at each consultation; several items defined each variable, and the two scales had coefficient alpha reliabilities of .82 and .73, respectively. Scores on these scales were converted to a 1-to-4 metric, where 1 meant low on the characteristic and 4 meant high on the characteristic.

Results

The results of our analyses are presented in two sections, corresponding to the two approaches outlined above for analyzing utilization: the level of the individual idea and the level of the consultation as a whole.

RESULTS AT THE LEVEL OF THE INDIVIDUAL IDEA

A total of 788 suggestions were rated in the 39 consultations. The frequency distribution of status scores for these ideas is presented in Table 1. Nineteen percent of the consultants' suggestions had been implemented as presented, and 6% had been implemented with adaptations. This gives an overall utilization percentage of 25.5% of the ideas; in other words, about one in four of the consultants' recommendations had been utilized. Another fourth of the suggestions had not been utilized: Nothing had been done about 16% of the ideas, and 9% had been considered and rejected. Almost 50% of the ideas fell in the middle utilization category, Interest in idea, at the time of the first follow-up; that is, the ideas had been neither fully implemented nor rejected.

The frequency distribution of difficulty scores is presented in Table 2. It can be seen that most ideas were in the moderate-to-low difficulty categories (9 and below) and that only about a third had difficulty scores of 10 and above. The correlations among the components of the difficulty measure are presented in Table 3. All were positive and significantly greater than zero. The level of intercorrelation among these is comparable to that among items combined in many multiitem scales in psychology.

Utilization scores and difficulty level were found to be significantly associated ($\chi 2$ = 83.40, p < .001). A summarization of the results of this crosstabulation is presented in Table 4. This table lists the percentage of ideas in each status category that had received each difficulty rating. The status category showing the clearest link to difficulty is "Implemented as presented." Relatively few of the ideas in this category were high in difficulty (9.2% had difficulty scores of 11 or higher) whereas many were low (51.6% had difficulty scores of 7 or less). Another status category related to difficulty was "Considered and rejected." Very few of the ideas that had been considered and rejected were easy to implement (i.e., had low difficulty), but relatively many were of intermediate difficulty. On the whole, ideas in the middle status categories—those in which there was interest but which had neither been fully utilized nor rejected—were more likely to be high in difficulty (22.6% were in difficulty categories 11 and above) than either ideas that had not been utilized (19.0%) or those that had been utilized (10.5%). This suggests that it takes longer for centers to come to decisions about difficult ideas.

TABLE 1: Frequencies and Percentages of Suggestions in Various Status Categories and Summary Categories at Four-Month Follow-Up

Status Category	N	Percent	Summary Category	N	Percent
1. Considered and rejected	72	9.1			
2. Nothing done	129	16.4	Non-utilization	201	25.5
3. Under consideration	152	19.3			
4. Steps taken	115	14.6	Interest in idea	386	49.0
5. Partially implemented	119	15.1			
6. Implemented as presented	152	19.3	Utilization	201	25.5
7. Implemented but adapted	49	6.2			

Note: N=788 suggestions

TABLE 2: Difficulty of Implementing Consultants' Suggestions
to Community Mental Health Centers

Difficulty	N	Percent
5	60	7.6
6	114	14.5
7	128	16.2
8	152	19.3
9	114	14.5
10	74	9.4
11	77	9.8
12	69	8.8
	778	100.00

TABLE 3: Correlations Among Components of
Difficulty of Consultants' Suggestions

	Cost	People	Effort	Trialability	Complexity
Cost	-				
People	.22*	-			
Effort	.31*	.38*	-		
Trialability	.32*	.15*	.28*	-	
Complexity	.31*	.23*	.35*	.36*	-

NOTE: N = 788 ideas
       *p < .001

RESULTS AT THE LEVEL OF A SET OF IDEAS

The number of suggestions noted in each consultation ranged from 6 to
34 (M = 20.2, SD = 7.5). Table 5 presents the percentage of consultant
suggestions in each summary category using the consultation as the level of

TABLE 4: Percentage of Ideas in Each Difficulty Category

Status Category	Difficulty							
	5	6	7	8	9	10	11	12
Considered and rejected	4.2	5.6	8.3	26.4	26.4	11.1	4.2	13.9
Nothing done	7.8	15.5	13.2	15.5	17.1	11.6	12.4	7.0
Under consideration	3.9	17.1	20.4	17.8	13.2	5.9	10.5	11.2
Steps taken	9.6	9.6	14.8	19.1	14.8	11.3	8.7	12.2
Partially implemented	5.0	10.1	18.5	21.8	10.9	8.4	16.0	9.2
Implemented as presented	14.5	21.1	16.4	22.4	8.6	7.9	6.6	2.6
Implemented but adapted	4.1	18.4	20.4	8.2	20.4	14.3	6.1	8.2

TABLE 5: Percent of Consultant Suggestions in Each Summary Category

Summary Category	Mean Percentage Score	SD	Range
Non-utilization	24.7	14.8	0-72
Interest in idea	50.3	14.9	21-87
Utilization	25.1	13.6	0-52
Overall utilization (combines utilization and non-utilization)	75.4	24.2	2-115

NOTE: N= 39 consultations

analysis. The percentage of ideas in the nonutilization category ranged from 0 to 72 (M = 24.7, SD = 14.8). The percentage in which there was interest but neither utilization nor nonutilization varied from 21 to 87 (M = 50.3, SD = 14.9). Utilization percentages ranged from 0 to 52 (M = 25.1, SD = 13.6). Scores on the overall utilization measure, which combines utilization and nonutilization percentages, varied from 2 to 115 (M = 75.4, SD = 24.2). Thus, it can be seen that there was quite a wide variation among the 39 consultations in centers' use of consultants' recommendations.

The mean score on consultants' encouragement of staff participation for the 39 consultations was 2.9 (SD = .7 on the 1-4 scale) and the mean knowledgeability score of the consultants was 3.7 (SD = .5). Thus consultants were seen as both encouraging staff to participate and highly knowledgeable. Despite these high average values, there was sufficient variability on scale scores among centers to permit them to be analyzed against the utilization measures. The correlations between these two scales and center utilization percentage scores are presented in Table 6. The table shows that degree of consultant encouragement of staff participation was not significantly related to centers' use of consultants' suggestions. Consultants' knowledgeability was positively related to overall utilization of their suggestions and negatively associated with degree of nonutilization. In other words, consultants who were more knowledgeable had more suggestions utilized than nonutilized and fewer suggestions not utilized than did consultants lower in knowledgeability.

TABLE 6: Correlations Between Consultant Characteristics and Summary Categories

| | Consultant Characteristic | |
Summary Category	Encourages Staff Participation	Knowledgeable
Non-utilization	-.06	-.32*
Interest in idea	.09	.15
Utilization	-.04	18
Overall utilization	.02	.29*

NOTE: One-tailed significance tests were used in this analysis
  *p < .05

DISCUSSION

This article has considered alternative forms of utilization and issues in their measurement. The research context for this analysis was a study of information utilization in 39 program-oriented consultations with community mental health center staff.

For the purposes of this study, utilization was considered not as an all-or-none phenomenon, but rather as a complex variable incorporating different types of utilization activities. Seven categories of utilization and nonutilization were developed and rated. Results indicated that all of the categories accounted for some portion of outcome, thus these categories may all be nontrivial ones in the study of information utilization in community mental health centers. It may also be the case, however, that these categories may not exhaust the range of utilization outcome in other organization settings, but rather that these categories reflect utilization occurring only in the research reported. Other categories may be proposed and their study may yield informative results.

The approach taken has emphasized the need for studying separately utilization of individual ideas and utilization of a set of ideas. The kinds of questions that may be asked at each level of analysis are different. In the former case, questions concerning characteristics of a particular bit of information are most appropriate; in the latter case, attention is focused on more global features of the situation in which information utilization occurs. Each of these orientations has its place in addressing questions about information utilization.

The question of scaling of utilization and of methods for combining utilization categories is one that warrants continued attention. The procedures of treating utilization categories as nominal or ordinal, of grouping them into superordinate categories, and of developing percentage variables to summarize utilization at the organizational level provided means of summarizing large amounts of data on utilization and have permitted testing hypotheses about the correlates of utilization. Whether these procedures are optimum ones for assessing utilization remains an open question. An important task for utilization researchers is development of methods for validating such categories. The approach we have used is an iterative one alternating between study of the relations among scores on utilization categories and examination of correlations between the categories and other measures. Other methods may be proposed, and it is anticipated that the task of assessing utilization will become clearer in the future.

In the illustrative results presented, suggestions that were easy to implement were found to be more readily utilized, and more difficult ideas were found in greater proportions in an intermediate state between utilization and nonutilization. Additionally, more difficult suggestions apparently were not the ones most likely to be rejected. This counterintuitive finding is examined in greater detail in analyses presented elsewhere. It was also found that the degree to which consultants encouraged staff participation bore little relation to utilization at a consultation, but that knowledgeable consultants did have relatively more of their suggestions implemented than did consultants lower in knowledgeability. These findings support the usefulness of separate assessment of utilization at the level of the individual ideas and at the level of a set of ideas.

REFERENCES

BERMAN, P. and M. W. McLAUGHLIN (1977) "Federal programs supporting educational change," in Factors Affecting Implementation and Continuation (Vol. 7). Santa Monica, CA: Rand.

CAMPEAU, P. L. et al (1978) "Evaluation of project information package dissemination and implementation." First year report. Palo Alto, CA: American Institutes for Research.

RYAN, B. and N. C. GROSS (1943) "The diffusion of hybrid seed corn in two Iowa communities." Rural Society 8: 15-24.

WEISS, C. H. [ed.] (1977) Using Social Research in Public Policy Making. Lexington, MA: Lexington Books.

5

MEASURING EVALUATION-INDUCED CHANGE IN MENTAL HEALTH PROGRAMS

Cathy D. Anderson
James A. Ciarlo
Susan F. Brodie

Mental Health Systems Evaluation Project
University of Denver
and
Denver Department of Health and Hospitals
Mental Health Program

The Services Improvement Project is a research effort funded by the National Institute of Mental Health. The focus of our study is a comparison of different styles of evaluation feedback in terms of the extent to which the information is utilized. We provide evaluation assistance to service elements of the Denver Department of Health and Hospitals Mental Health Program, and in exchange for this evaluation resource, the service units assist us in allowing us to assess the extent of utilization of the feedback we offer.

Our present research design requires that we work with several similar service units simultaneously on the same evaluation problem. We present regular feedback on our research and data analyses at the units' staff meetings, systematically varying our style of feedback across the service teams. Currently, we offer three modes of data feedback: special, causal-correlational, and options feedback. Options feedback may be regarded as the most statistically sophisticated of these. It includes graphic or tabular presentation of contrasts and subgroups, presentation of the results of statistical analyses and their significance levels, and cost/outcome options analysis whenever possible. The cost/outcome analysis contrasts various policy or practice options in terms of the projected potential advantages

AUTHORS' NOTE: We are indebted to James M. Weyant, Ph.D., and Frank J. Javorek, Ph.D., for their contributions to our procedures for utilization assessment.

and disadvantages of each. Causal-correlational feedback includes the tabular or graphic data presentation and statistical significance testing only. Results usually indicate what team-controllable practices may be involved in observed outcomes. Our special feedback condition is intended to allow a team to get involved with the data relevant to a problem with a minimum of statistical analysis. Our feedback to a team in this condition includes tabular presentation of descriptive information about subgroups. In addition to these three conditions, we also have a control group. A team in this condition receives no data feedback on the issue being evaluated, other than what might be available in the context of routine monthly and annual statistical reports.

The remainder of this article discusses the manner in which we assess utilization of our different types of feedback. This includes a description of our utilization interview, the assessment process, and a brief summary of our past and present work in measuring utilization.

THE INTERVIEWS

The principal tool used by our project to assess utilization is a series of structured interviews. Members of the service teams are interviewed prior to any evaluation intervention ("preintervention interview") and at one-month and six-month intervals following the completion of the intervention.

Preintervention Interview

The preintervention interview serves four specific aims for utilization assessment. First, we collect information from each team member on what he/she believes is causing or contributing to the situation or problem under investigation, together with the individual's ideas about possible solutions. This information is used to generate the "content themes" which are used to assess cognitive change; these will be discussed later in this report.

The second goal of the preinterview is to collect data on the current status of the issue in terms of team problem-solving activities. We ask each individual what the team is currently doing to deal with the issue and also what he/she perceives to be obstacles impeding solution. This information guides us in formulating research hypotheses for the team, in choosing fruitful resources to examine in our analyses, and in later differentiating problem-solving activities that are probably results of our evaluation intervention from extant activities.

Our preinterview is also used to help select a panel for the two postinterviews. In many cases the service team involved in our evaluation is large, and it is neither convenient for us nor acceptable to the team for us to interview all members. During the preinterview, each team member is questioned about individuals on his/her team who are particularly concerned about the issue, who are important or influential in solving problems, or who may be exceptionally knowledgeable about it. We use these "endorsements" along with information on the formal leadership of the team to select a panel of approximately 7 to 10 individuals. The two postinterviews are conducted with these panel members only.

The final goal of our preinterview represents a recent addition to our utilization assessment. In our next intervention we will be collecting "pre-" data from each team member on his/her feelings vis-à-vis the issue being investigated. Specifically, we will be asking each individual to rate his/her concern about the issue (extremely, somewhat, or not at all concerned; or other affect) and his/her satisfaction with the way the team is now handling the issue (5-point scale ranging from very satisfied to very dissatisfied). We feel that various combinations of these two affective items may be useful predictors of later utilization. For example, if team members are predominantly extremely concerned about an issue and also very dissatisfied with the way that they are currently dealing with it, they may be more likely to utilize evaluation feedback than a team that is predominantly not concerned and/or satisfied with current solutions. In addition to the predictive potential of these two items, they also will be used to assess impact on utilization. This will be discussed further in the second section of this article.

The Postintervention Interviews

The postintervention interviews are conducted at one- and six-month intervals following the completion of an evaluation study. During these interviews we again ask about the status of the problem in terms of changes in actions, practices, or policies. We also ask about changes or constraints elsewhere in the mental health center or local mental health system that may have a bearing on the issue. We also ask respondents to rate their present feelings about the issue and their views on its causes and possible solutions. The manner in which this information is collected and interpreted will be described next.

UTILIZATION ASSESSMENT

For the purpose of assessment, we have conceptualized utilization in terms of three traditional psychological dimensions: behavioral, cognitive, and affective. Currently, the data for measuring all three of these dimensions are collected in the panel members' interviews, although we will cross-check responses using archival or other materials when feasible.

Behavioral Change

We measure behavioral change by examining reported changes in the team's activities, practices, or policies that resulted from our evaluation intervention. In the past, these data were collected from panel members' responses to two questions in our one-month and six-month postinterviews. The first of these questions we call our "open-ended" measure. We ask each panel member to describe specific instances of any activities that he/she or the team has undertaken with regard to the issue being studied. In our second, "recommendation-cued" measure, we read each respondent a list of the recommendations we made in our final report to the team and again asked them to cite specific instances of activities relevant to the recommendation.

We had several reasons for obtaining these two measures (open-ended and recommendation-cued) of behavioral utilization. The open-ended format has the advantage of being comparable across both experimental and control groups. That is, it allows us to compare the problem-solving activities of a team for which we have completed an evaluation intervention to those activities of a team that has received no data feedback on the problem. An additional advantage to the open-ended procedure is that it is probably less susceptible to the demand characteristics of the utilization interview situation; that is, this may minimize the tendency of a respondent to report that the team followed our recommendations just to make the exchange with the interviewer more cordial. The cued procedure is advantageous because it often helps the respondent to recall activities that are not current or particularly outstanding or salient; the disadvantage of this, however, is that for some respondents it may be difficult to acknowledge that no activities have resulted from a specific recommendation.

For the reasons just reviewed, we regarded the open-ended and the recommendation-cued items in our interview as complementary. Respondents were always asked first to report utilization activities in the open-ended manner described above and then to respond specifically to each recommendation. In the future, however, we will be substituting a "result" cued item for the recommendation-cued one. We feel that this procedure will have all the advantages of the recommendation-cued item and it will not preclude reporting activities that resulted from the evaluation intervention in ways other than those that we recommended or expected.

After the interviewing phase of utilization assessment is completed, at least two members of our research staff review condensed transcripts of these interviews. They extract (separately for both the open-ended and cued items) representative statements and a list of respondents who produced them. Next, these items are coded by category of utilization represented. Our coding scheme allows us to classify the statements according to several dimensions—feedback relevant versus feedback irrelevant activities, feedback compatible (utilization) versus feedback incompatible uses, and, within these distinctions, qualitative differences in the types of utilization reported. Table 1 presents the utilization categories and codes currently used by our project.

It should be noted that our coding schema has undergone substantial revision as our project has progressed. These revisions reflect several aims. First, after each set of interviews is completed and coded, we compute a measure of the interrater reliability of our coding. We constantly attempt to clarify and refine our codes to improve upon this reliability. In addition, we would like each code to be mutually exclusive with respect to all other codes. Finally, we tried to have a comprehensive set of codes; that is, each representative statement extracted from our interviews should be codable, and the codes should be sensitive in terms of discriminating differences in activities that are relevant to utilization assessment.

TABLE 1: Schema for Coding Behavioral Utilization

Category Code Number[1]	Description
1	New action, practice or policy *implemented* or pre-existing action, practice or policy *intensified.*
2	Pre-existing actions, policies or practices *terminated* or *diminished.*
3	Change in actions, practices or policies *decided on, but not yet implemented.*
4	Solutions or improvements in action, practice or policy seriously considered or initiated but *rejected* or *aborted* because of *valid* reasons (e.g., external constraints, not feasible).
5	Active decision to *maintain the status quo*, including abandoning pre-existing plans for change.
6	Change in action, practice, or policy *casually considered* but not seriously pursued.
7	*Rejected* or *misunderstood* the data and its implications.
8	*No evidence of serious consideration* of the data.

[1] For codes 1-6, attach an "A" if the feedback data seem to have suggested the action, practice, policy or change; if not, attach a "B".

It sometimes occurs that respondents report on similar events but the contents of their reports are contradictory. For cases such as these, we have established a method for reconciling differences. A staff member who is familiar with the organizational structure of the teams is told that two individuals have presented conflicting reports. He is also told the position that each individual holds on the team. Without knowing which specific report is attributed to a given individual, he then judges (based on the position an individual holds) which team member would be most likely to provide reliable information on the teams activities and policies, and that person's statement is selected as the more representative one.

When we have completed the steps described above, we have a set of utilization-coded, representative statements and a list of the respondents who endorsed them. This is one of the measures that we use to compare utilization activities, decisions, and policies between teams. We regard our coding schema as identifying nominal categories; therefore, our team comparisons are actually more descriptive than statistical in nature. For later studies we have added an additional item to our interviews that will allow us also to make quantitative comparisons of behavioral utilization. We will ask each respondent to rate on an anchored scale the extent to which changes in actions, practices, policies, and decisions have resulted from the evaluation intervention. We will present these scaled ratings both in the open-ended and the result cued contexts.

Cognitive Change

The information collected in the preintervention interview on the respondents views about the nature of the issue and its solutions is used to extract "content themes." When all of the preintervention interviews are completed, similar themes are combined, and the result is a list of succinct statements reflecting beliefs about various aspects of the issue we are studying. This list of original content themes is then taken to a team in an early meeting, and each individual team member is asked to rate his/her agreement with each theme, using a 5-point scale (ranging from strong agreement to strong disagreement). In addition to these initial themes, our subsequent research generates a list of "data themes," or statements concerning some aspect of the issue for which we have provided data analysis and feedback. In some cases, an original theme may also become a data theme; that is, we may feedback data on some aspect of the problem about which team members originally held opinions. Their initial view may then be either confirmed or disconfirmed by our data feedback.

At one-month and six-month intervals after the completion of our evaluation intervention, we ask the panel members to again rate their agreement with the themes, both initial themes and data themes. For initial themes, we can examine change over three points in time (perintervention and one-month and six-months postintervention). These trends should allow us to test a variety of hypotheses about evaluation utilization. For example, does feedback generate detectable cognitive changes? Is there decay of information after evaluation-initiated change? We can also check for any temporal relationship between cognitive changes and behavioral change as reflected in our other measures.

For data themes not originally generated in the preintervention interview, we can examine whether the postevaluation views of the panel are in agreement or in conflict with the data we presented.

Affective Change

Our project has recently begun to assess affective change. Each panel member will rate his or her concern about the problem or issue and his/her satisfaction with the team's solutions. These ratings will be made at the preintervention interview and at the two postintervention interviews. As mentioned previously, we will attempt to predict utilization from preintervention interview responses to these items. We will also measure affective change over time and examine the relationship between behavioral, affective, and cognitive change following evaluation feedback.

As is probably apparent from the foregoing discussion, one feature of our utilization assessment is that we are frequently modifying and amplifying it to reflect difficulties and opportunities for improvement of the clarity, reliability, and validity of our measures. The initial utilization study described later represents our first steps in this developmental process.

How Does Our Assessment of Utilization Compare to that of Other Investigators?

The interview is our principal instrument for collecting assessment data. Our interview protocol differs from that used in several other investigations in that it assesses utilization in more than one way. With our recommendations-cued and our cognitive change items, we assess the extent to which the service unit has complied with recommendations and/or changed their beliefs in accordance with our study findings. Our open-ended items on behavioral change and our assessment of affective change are more content-free, however. That is, they are applicable to a variety of problem-solving or policy-setting situations and are potentially sensitive to change other than that which might be directly predictable from our intervention. In contrast, Fairweather, Tornatzsky, and Fergus (see Fergus, 1979) use a change score as their dependent measure of utilization. Each item in their interview enumerates a particular element of programmatic change, and the question is essentially, "Has it been done?" A difficulty with this procedure is that it limits the scope of measured utilization to those specific activities that the evaluator expected or recommended as a consequence of the intervention. This is essentially the criticism that Rich (1978: 105) makes of what he calls "input/output analysis" of utilization. When an investigator attempts to trace the manner in which specific bits of information are used in decision making, he or she is essentially measuring "instrumental" utilization. Rich distinguishes this from "conceptual" utilization which is more difficult to associate with specific inputs. There are often indirect or unpredicted associations found between input and subsequent changes, which Rich attributes to the fact that "policy is not made, it accumulates." We are attempting to assess this indirect utilization by providing an open-ended (in the sense that the activities reported need not be directly responsive to our recommendations) assessment of behavior change as well as a relatively long follow-up period (six months) which potentially would allow us to observe more indirect and delayed changes.

Other investigators do share our goal of attempting to broaden the scope of what is considered to be utilization. Larsen (1979) asks "whether there are basic concepts of utilization that apply as well to non-policy oriented settings as to policy-oriented ones. Examples of such concepts might be conceptual versus instrumental utilization; long-term and short-term utilization; enlightenment; challenge to the status quo; exactly what constitutes utilization, and the like." Similarly, Patton (1978: 23-35) uses the interview procedure to extract quotes that reflect "non-program impact" as well as programmatic change. Our utilization assessment differs from these two investigators, however, in the manner in which we evaluate these examples once they are extracted. From Patton's description of his 1975 utilization assessment studies, it appears that once he extracts representative statements, they are primarily used in a descriptive and anecdotal manner to illustrate the extent and nature of utilization. Larsen, on the other hand, assigns codes to her examples of utilization, as is done in our project. However, a principal difference between her approach and ours is that her codes appear to reflect an ordinal scale of measurement. We prefer to be more conservative and treat our codes as categorical or nominal, because we feel that, depending on the actual content of an activity, there may be considerable within-code differences in scope (in terms of problem-solving efforts or progress). We are also not assured that some types of behavior (e.g., adding a new practice) should be considered as indicating greater utilization than others (e.g., increasing an already existing practice). For these reasons, we prefer to let our findings "speak more for themselves." Larsen deals with the problem of equivalence within codes by evaluating a "scope/quality" dimension within her utilization codes.

I was not intended that this section be a comprehensive comparison of our approach to utilization assessment and that of other investigations. It is hoped, however, that some of what we feel to be the more salient differences in our approach are evident. The following section of this report presents a review of our first utilization assessment.

THE "CHRONIC PATIENT" PROBLEM

The data for our first utilization assessment came from evaluation studies that we conducted for two inpatient service units in the Denver Department of Health and Hospitals Mental Health Program, the Adult Psychiatric Inpatient Service and the In-hospital Alcoholism Detoxification service. Guided by the interests of the team and the scope of our data base, our evaluation focused on effectiveness of policies regarding treatment of chronic patients. The directions taken by our subsequent analyses differed across the two teams.

For the Psychiatric service, our first step was to define the "chronic" patient and to feed back data to the staff on the extent of the problem and possible dimensions which differentiate chronics from "nonchronics." Next, we examined service utilization by chronic patients, focusing on average length and number of inpatient episodes and the relationship of recidivism and ward census. We then addressed the implications of several treatment variables (length of treatment, psychiatric after care, transfer to a long-term treatment facility, and after-care medications) on such outcome measures as probability of recidivism, time to readmission, and outcome scores on a multidimensional client outcome measure, the Denver Community Mental Health Questionnaire. This evaluation study resulted in eight recommendations to the staff.

We also begin by clarifying the definition of chronicity for the Alcoholism service and describing the extent of the chronic patient problem there. Next, we examined the relationship of several treatment variables (length of stay, postdischarge antiabuse program referrals, patient involvement in outpatient antiabuse programs, and the impact of an alcohol education program) on treatment outcomes. As was the case with the psychiatric service, we fed back the results of these analyses, and our evaluation culminated in a list of five recommendations that we presented to the ward staff. In addition to the statistical feedback and recommendations, we also performed and presented two "option evaluations" for the alcoholism staff. The first of these examined the costs and outcomes of patient involvement in antiabuse treatment programs; the second compared the costs and outcomes of three alternative referral patterns for monitored antiabuse.

Following completion of the feedback process, we presented final reports to both teams and then conducted one-month and six-month postintervention interviews at the appropriate intervals. The results of this utilization assessment are described below.

Behavioral Assessment—One-Month Postintervention Interviews

Table 2 presents the recommendations that we offered to the two units. Tables 3 and 4 contain the representative utilization statements extracted from the open-ended items of the one-month postintervention interviews for the psychiatric unit and the alcohol unit, respectively, together with the assigned codes presented in Table 1. We were not using a recommendation-cued item at the time of our one-month interviews. Two independent coders extracted these statements from condensed interview transcripts. The overall intercoder agreement for statement extraction on the open-ended item of the one-month postinterview was 65% for the psychiatric unit and 85% for the alcohol unit. These percentages were calculated by dividing the number of commonly extracted statements by the total list of representative statements. Most disagreement, however, occurred in statements which did not reflect utilization, that is, statements that eventually were coded as 1b, 2b, 3b, 4b, 5b, 6b, 7, or 8. When only statements reflecting some utilization are considered (1a, 2a, 3a, 4a, 5a, 6a) the agreement for extraction was 83% for the psychiatric unit and 100% for the alcohol unit on the one-month open-ended item. Whenever disagreement occurred, it was reconciled by discussion and/or the decision of a third coder.

The process of extracting statements for coding involves sifting out relevant statements from copious irrelevant material. Not surprisingly, it appears that when the activities reported are related to the issue that was studied, but were judged to *not* be a result of the study, the most ambiguity results. Fortunately, this is not a severe problem for utilization assessment as described here because the lack of agreement does not

TABLE 2: "Chronic Patient" Study Recommendations

A. Recommendations to Alcoholism Detoxification Service

1. Meet to clarify with all staff the magnitude of the chronic patient problem (e.g., most patients are chronic, and many—about 1/3—will be readmitted to inpatient care).
2. Patient stays should be no longer than necessary for detoxification and discharge planning.
3. Increase the number of discharged patients who get involved in monitored antabuse programs, to a goal of 35% of the service's patients.
4. Oppose any phase-out of the service's monitored antabuse program, and attempt to refer all of the service's dischargees to its own antabuse program.
5. Abandon possible plans to initiate an on-ward education program involving an increased ward stay.

B. Recommendations to Psychiatric Inpatient Service

1. Meet to clarify with *all* staff the size of the ward's chronic patient population and effects of ward discharge policies on readmissions. (Fewer chronic than acute patients; neither a high ward census nor early discharge cause readmissions.)
2. Plan ahead for an increasing percentage of chronic patients in the future.
3. High risk patient stays should be no longer than necessary for safe, minimal levels of functioning, unless an extended stay is aimed specifically at employment-related goals.
4. On-ward treatment programs should be modified to include employment-related activites.
5. Additional resources should be sought to allow moderately longer stays for high-risk patients to further improve their in-community productivity.
6. Meet with psychopharmacologists and aftercare clinicians to review possible negative effects on productivity of large dosages of major tranquilizer plus anti-Parkinsonism drugs.
7. Meet with aftercare clinicians to discuss the effects of aftercare counseling, both positive (on Productivity) and negative (on Psychological Distress).
8. Discuss use of the State hospital as a referral source during high ward census periods, since referral there does not increase the probability of readmission.

usually extend to statements describing activities that *do* reflect utilization.

Once the statements were extracted, they were coded. The intercoder agreement rate was 69% for the psychiatric unit and 64% for the alcohol unit. Again, discrepancies were resolved by adding a third opinion. Table 5 provides a summary of the behavioral utilization of the two teams. It appears from this table that the psychiatric unit, which received only

TABLE 3: Summary of Behavioral Utilization (One-Month Post-Intervention) for Psychiatric Inpatient Service: "Chronic Patient" Study

Representative Statements	Assigned Utilization Code
We have been recommending on discharge forms that medication doses be tapered.	1a
We have been putting more emphasis on work productivity.	1a
Residents have been told to get an occupational history on each patient.	1a
We have gone out to one out-patient team and we plan to go to all of them to increase coordination.	1a
We are attempting to coordinate with other mental health agencies in our system.	1a
Hospital attendants have been upgraded to "program attendants".	1b
We have been exploring the legal system for better ways of helping clients.	1b
We have initiated a program for following-up high risk patients.	1b
We are sending some patients to the activity center.	1b
We have a new referral source, a local nursing home.	1b
We are increasing our orientation toward training and education.	1b
We have been keeping patients longer.	7

"causal/correlation" feedback, more actively engaged in problem-solving activities (as indicated by the frequencies of codes 1a, 2a, 3a, 4a, 5a, and 6a) than the alcoholism unit, which also received "option evaluation" feedback on several issues. This type of comparison may be misleading, however. The teams may have differed at the beginning of this study in organizational characteristics which would be expected to influence their activity level. In addition, the recommendations that we made probably differ in ease of acceptance and utilization. Possible ways of dealing with these problems will be discussed below.

TABLE 4: Summary of Behavioral Utilization (One-Month Post-Intervention) for Alcoholism Detoxification Service: "Chronic Patient" Study

Representative Statements	Assigned Utilization Code
We have been working harder on encouraging all people for monitored antabuse.	1a
We put less emphasis on the location of a patient's residence in referring them for monitored antabuse; we try to have everyone come back to this service for it.	1a
The Sobriety Chip program is being revitalized.	1b
We have four new staff members.	1b
We are trying to do more educational programs and to increase our communication with other facilities.	1b
We are providing more patient education.	1b
We are trying to individualize programs for patients.	1b
Patients are shown more empathy.	1b
We have more inservice training planned.	3a
We disregarded our plan to create an extended therapy program.	5a
We once discussed ways to increase the volume of monitored antabuse, but decided that we can't do anything that we're not already doing.	6a
We were thinking about a county-farm for chronic patients, but it doesn't seem feasible.	6b

Behavioral Utilization–Six-Month Postintervention Interviews

We followed the same procedure described above to assess behavioral utilization six months after our evaluation feedback had ended. In addition, the recommendation-cued item was added to our six-month interviews in an attempt to generate greater precision in reporting utilization.

For the open-ended item, the agreement in extracting statements was 73% for the psychiatric unit and 66.7% for the alcohol unit. When only statements that were subsequently coded as utilization are considered, however, the rates increase to 100% agreement for the psychiatric ward

TABLE 5: Comparison of One-Month Post-Intervention Behavioral Utilization Activities" the "Chronic Patient" Study

Utilization Category	Psychiatric Inpatient Service	Alcohol Detoxification Service
1A	We recommend tapering medications after discharge.	We are working harder to get patients into monitored antabuse after discharge.
	We emphasize improving work productivity.	We are referring fewer people to antabuse services, and instead requesting that they return to our unit.
	Residents now take an occupational history on each patient (to facilitate therapeutic plan for work productivity).	
	We have visited one out-patient team and plan to visit others to facilitate continuity of aftercare.	
	We are trying to increase coordination with other agencies in our system.	
	We are bringing comprehensive evaluations and occupational therapy evaluations on chronics to outpatient teams.	
2A	—	—
3A	—	We are planning more inservice training related to chronic patients.
4A	—	—
5A	—	—
6A	—	We discussed ways to improve the number of patients accepting monitored antabuse after discharge; we couldn't come up with any ways other than what we are currently doing.

and 83% for the alcohol unit. The percentage agreement in coding these statements was 88 for the psychiatric ward and 100 for the alcohol unit.

On the recommendation-cued question, the agreement in extracting representative statements was 50% for the psychiatric unit. Again, this percentage is increased considerably (88%) when only statements representing utilization are considered. The percentage agreement for the alcohol unit on statement extraction for the recommendation-cued question was 87.5%. The percentage agreement in coding all statements was 100% for the psychiatric unit and 71% for the alcohol unit.

Table 6 compares the utilization activities for the two teams as reflected by both the open-ended and the cued questions in the six-month postinterview. Again, the psychiatric unit reported more utilization activities than did the alcohol unit; but the differences in the scope of these activities makes comparison on a quantitative basis difficult. For example, four of the six activities coded as intensified activity (1A) on the open-ended question for the psychiatric unit involve *discussion*; but, the two activities mentioned in the same item by the alcohol team represent *policy changes*. While we could increase the number of different categories to accommodate these differences, we might lower our reliability of scoring as well.

It is interesting to note that, as expected, the number of activities reported by the psychiatric team increased markedly on the cued questions. This was not the case, however, for the alcohol unit. Unfortunately, we cannot determine whether there were more activities of relatively low salience that the cued question elicited for the psychiatric team or whether the differences are due to differences in the unit's sensitivities to the demand characteristics discussed earlier.

Cognitive Change

At one-month and six-month intervals following our evaluation intervention, we asked the staff of both units to rate their agreement on a list of statements about the chronic patient problem.

These statements, or themes, are presented in Tables 7 and 8 for the psychiatric unit and the alcohol unit, respectively. Statements were of three types: statements about which we presented feedback data, statements that team members made during initial interviews but about which no evaluation study was pursued, and "filler" statements relevant to the problem but about which we presented no data. For each statement that

TABLE 6: Comparison of Six-Month Post-Intervention Behavioral Utilization Activities:
The "Chronic Patient" Study

A. Open-Ended Report

Utilization Category	Psychiatric Inpatient Service	Alcohol Detoxification Service
1A	We now have an individual responsible for coordination of outpatient care. We have begun weekly discussions about the care of chronics. We have been conferring more with outpatient teams.	We are pushing harder to get discharged patients involved in monitored antabuse.
2A	—	We have been decreasing our referrals to other sites for monitored antabuse and seeing more patients here.
3A	—	
4A	We tried to increase communication with outpatient teams, but they are resistant.	
5A	—	The results of the study confirmed our positive feelings about monitored antabuse; we are continuing our emphasis on it.
6A	—	We considered requiring antabuse for admission, but we didn't think it would work.

TABLE 6 (Continued)

	B. Cued Report	
Utilization Category	Psychiatric Inpatient Service	Alcohol Detoxification Service
1A	We bring up the findings about length of stay when we discuss patient planning.	
	We had a meeting to discuss the results of the study.	
	We have increased our emphasis on outpatient continuity of care.	
	We cite the study when we are considering extended stays for vocational rehabilitation purposes.	
	Our ward got two extra beds and more increases are planned.	
	In meetings and orientation we discuss the negative effects of drugs and encourage tapering medications.	
2A		—
3A	We are planning to meet with the State Hospital to discuss problems with referrals.	
4A	We are attempting to involve aftercare teams more, but there's resistance.	—
5A	—	We have continued opposing the phase-out of our on-ward antabuse program.
		We have abandoned plans for an on-ward education program.
		We accepted the results of the study and continued to have short stays for most patients.
6A	—	—

114

TABLE 7: Alcohol Detoxification Unit: Themes to be
Rated on the "Chronic Patient" Problem

* 1. The readmission rate of chronic patients is very high.
* 2. Only a small proportion of patients, one out of ten, readmit within a year.
* 3. Three or more readmissions in two years are rare (less than 5%).
  4. Lack of placements in the community causes no improvement and readmission.
* 5. Length of stay on the ward has very little effect on the personal and social functioning of the patient.
* 6. Patients need a longer stay to prevent their readmission.
* 7. Time for patient therapy is too short and causes a lack of effective treatment with no improvement.
  8. We don't know what to do with chronic patients.
  9. Patients are treated impersonally which causes no improvement.
  10. Lack of staff cohesion causes lack of effective treatment and no patient improvement.
  11. A solution to the chronic patient problem is to require participation in monitored antabuse after discharge.
*12. Antabuse participation after discharge keeps more patients from readmitting.
*13. Antabuse participation extends in–community time between discharge and later readmission.
*14. The particular program at which a patient received antabuse makes no difference in readmission or time to readmission.
*15. Referral completions to our own Antabuse Program are higher than to another neighborhood program.
  16. Patient unwillingness to change and their low motivation causes poor staff attitudes.
  17. Lack of long-term treatment causes a high rate of return visits.
  18. A solution to the chronic patient problem is a "county farm" type of treatment facility.
*19. Participation in the state hospital Alcoholism Education Program did reduce later readmissions to our ward.
  20. We are doing the job of detoxification that the ward is set up for.

---

* Themes about which data feedback was presented.

was data relevant, an expected value (of agreement or disagreement) consistent with the results of our data feedback was selected for comparison with actual responses. These values, along with the average ratings given by panel members at one-month and six-months postintervention interviews, appear in Table 9.

It is apparent from reviewing Table 9 that agreement with our feedback (as reflected by ratings on relevant statements) is quite low for both units. The agreement rate at the psychiatric unit is 40% at one month and 50% at

TABLE 8: Psychiatric Inpatient Service: Themes to be Rated on the "Chronic Patient" Problem

* 1.   High ward census causes patients to be discharged too soon.

  2.   Open-door admission policy for chronic patients causes high census.

* 3.   Patients who are discharged too soon from the state hospital return to our ward more quickly.

* 4.   Referral to the state hospital does not affect either returning to our ward or the time to readmission to our ward.

  5.   The high readmission of chronic patients is caused by inadequate referral facilities.

  6.   Patients failure to take prescribed medication causes high readmission of chronic patients.

* 7.   The nature of the diagnosed illness causes high readmission of chronic patients.

  8.   High readmission of chronic patients is the result of inadequate follow-up and aftercare.

* 9.   Patient readmission is caused by patients being discharged too soon on the previous stay.

 10.   Too little attention to chronic patients on the ward causes high readmission.

 11.   Poor continuity of care produces high readmission of chronic patients.

*12.   Aftercare contacts prevent readmission of chronic patients.

*13.   The proportion of patients returning to the ward many times is very high.

 14.   There really never has been a problem with chronic patients on this ward.

 15.   The solution to the chronic patient problem is long-term institutionalization.

 16.   More resources, such as more beds and staff, would solve the problem of handling chronic patients.

 17.   Ward staff are frustrated with chronic patients because treatment doesn't seem to work.

*18.   Readmitted patients stay about the same length of time on our ward as first admissions.

*19.   High dosages of major tranquilizers have no effect on keeping patients in the community longer.

*20.   High dosages of major tranquilizers may reduce patient distress, but may also increase their dependence on welfare.

---

* Themes about which data feedback was presented.

---

six months; these rates are 36% at both follow-up points on the alcohol unit. Unfortunately, we do not have prefeedback ratings for these statements and, therefore, it is not possible to determine how much change in attitude occurred over this time period. A very low postevaluation rate of agreement may reflect cognitive change from extremely opposing preevaluation views or may reflect no change at all.

Although it is difficult to obtain much more than suggestive information about the extent of cognitive utilization in the absence of information

TABLE 9: Ratings for Data Themes

Psychiatric Inpatient Service

Statement	Expected Value[1]	$\bar{X}$ 1 Month	$\bar{X}$ 6 Months	Agreement with Data 1 Mo.	6 Mo.
1	< 3	3.00	3.70	No	No
3	< 3	3.40	3.86	No	No
4	> 3	2.90	2.43	No	No
7	> 3	4.30	3.86	Yes	Yes
9	< 3	2.50	2.43	Yes	Yes
12	> 3	4.30	3.29	No	No
13	< 3	3.00	3.57	No	No
18	> 3	2.80	3.29	No	Yes
19	< 3	2.40	2.14	Yes	Yes
20	> 3	3.40	3.43	Yes	Yes

Alcohol Detoxification Service

Statement	Expected Value[1]	X 1 Month	X 6 Months	Agreement with Data 1 Mo.	6 Mo.
1	< 3	3.50	3.60	No	No
2	> 3	2.50	2.20	No	No
3	> 3	2.20	2.80	No	No
5	> 3	3.00	3.20	No	Yes
6	< 3	2.80	3.60	Yes	No
7	< 3	3.00	3.60	No	No
12	> 3	3.80	4.00	Yes	Yes
13	> 3	4.00	3.80	Yes	Yes
14	> 3	2.00	2.00	No	No
15	> 3	4.00	3.20	Yes	Yes
19	< 3	2.70	2.60	Yes	Yes

[1] = Strongly Disagree, 3 = Neutral, 5 = Strongly Agree. A theme that was supported by our data would be expected to be rated > 3; a theme that was not supported, < 3.

about team members' initial opinions, it is of interest to compare the absolute amount of cognitive change from one-month and six-month postintervention between the feedback statements and the nonfeedback statements.

Table 10 compares the absolute change in ratings between the one-month and the six-month interviews for feedback and nonfeedback themes. It appears that the absolute value (either in the direction of more agreement or less agreement) of cognitive change is small and that it does not appear to be substantially different for the statements for which data feedback was provided than for nondata statements. In addition, if directional change as opposed to absolute change is considered, specifically change in data statements that is in the direction of our evaluation feedback, the results are again discouraging. Only 10% of the absolute cognitive change from one-month to six-months (measured by ratings of our themes) was in the direction of data feedback for the psychiatric team; 25.7% of the change for the alcohol unit was in this direction. Again, in the absence of information about initial attitudes, it is not possible to determine whether this reflects little or no change as a direct result of data feedback or if it indicates decay effects in earlier change that was in the direction of our feedback.

When one examines agreement on these themes in light of the content of the themes, some interesting observations emerge. There was a tendency for data conclusions to be rejected when a current ward situation could be viewed as contradictory. For example, on the psychiatric ward at the time of the postinterviews, the census was quite high and a usual disposition resource, the state hospital, was not open to them because of similar overload problems. Team members tended to reject statements reflecting that the proportion of chronic repeaters was not large and that the consequences of using the state hospital were not undesirable. Another tendency that appears is that of oversimplification. We presented the alcohol unit with several different findings concerning antiabuse, for example, that it increases time between readmission but does not decrease total recidivism. The ratings that they gave to statements about antiabuse reflect that what they retained was that antiabuse was beneficial, and this was generalized to all possible consequences of monitored antiabuse. Similarly, referring patients to alternate after-care facilities for antiabuse was generalized as an unfavorable outcome in certain respects not supported by our data.

We have planned several methodological changes that will allow us to make more definitive comparisons of cognitive change and the nature of

TABLE 10: Mean Absolute Changes in Ratings for Feedback Related and Non-Feedback Related Themes from One-Month to Six-Months Post-Intervention

	Data Themes	Non-Data Themes
Psychiatric Inpatient Service	.45	.39
Alcohol Detoxification Service	.31	.60

Note: The numbers in these cells reflect mean absolute (either in the direction of increased agreement or decreased agreement) change in ratings.

that change over time. One of these is to obtain preintervention ratings of content themes. Additional changes will be discussed further below.

Affective Change

Assessing affecting change as a possible reflection of the impact of evaluation intervention represents a new focus for our project. As discussed above, in the future we will be collecting ratings on staff concern and satisfaction prior to our evaluation study and at one-month and six-month intervals following the study. During the six-month postinterview of the drop-out study, we began asking panel members about their feelings concerning the problem. From this open-ended question, two dimensions—concern about the issue and satisfaction with its status—emerged as most salient. Of the seven panel members interviewed on the psychiatric unit, five described their affect as discouraged, concerned, upset, and frustrated. Two others described themselves as tired, not upset, "burned out." The alcohol unit staff members expressed similar feelings, describing themselves as depressed, concerned, not optimistic, "burned out." Adding a procedure for assessing affective change to our subsequent studies will allow us to examine whether evaluation feedback can improve upon or change feelings about a significant problem.

METHODOLOGICAL ISSUES

Difficulties that we experienced interpreting some of the data mentioned above have suggested several methodological changes that we plan to incorporate into future interventions.

One problem concerned the validity of comparing behavioral utilization solely on the basis of the number of activities reported and the codes assigned to these activities. Often activities that were assigned the same code differed in scope or ease of implementation. In order to reduce this problem we plan to exert more control over the scope of the problem being studied. In the past, problems were defined quite globally, for example, the "chronic patient" problem. We allowed the interests of the individual units to determine the specific direction in which our investigation would proceed. In the future we will try to select *relationships* to investigate that are of interest to all of the units involved. For example, we might study the relationship of length of treatment to various patient outcomes. This approach focuses the scopes of the problem, such that what we are investigating for each team is more similar and thus more comparable.

We will also eliminate specific *recommendations* for dealing with the problem for two reasons. First, without them the units can develop their *own* strategies for working on the problem, rather than ours. This potentially provides a more realistic and multidimensional picture of utilization activities than does an essentially yes or no response to whether a recommendation of ours was followed. A second advantage is that it will help to accentuate the differences between our three feedback modes. Only in the "options" feedback have we actually evaluated the implications of various solutions. Also, offering a specific recommendation to a "special feedback" group implies that the differences that we can observe in our breakdown summaries are actually statistically significant, whereas we prefer to avoid this interpretation if possible.

Three other methodological changes have been planned for future interventions. We will be adding a quantitative rating of behavioral utilization; panel members will be asked to select from a series of scaled alternatives the best description of the extent to which changes in practices and policies have resulted from our evaluation study. As noted earlier, our content themes will be rated before the evaluation intervention as well as after, to allow us to examine changes in affect over time. In addition, because the problems that we investigate will be more similar across the units than was the case in the past, the cognitive change dimension of our utilization assessment should also be more comparable. Finally, we will be scaling our affective questions as described earlier in this article and presenting these items both "pre-" and "post"-intervention. The "pre"- responses will hopefully allow us to predict future utilization, and the "pre- versus post-" comparisons will allow us to measure affective change as a function of evaluation feedback.

CONCLUSION

We have tried to illustrate here in considerable detail how we are conceptualizing, measuring, and analyzing the utilization of actual evaluation feedback by mental health service program managers and clinicians.

Some of our conclusions up to this point are listed here for the reader's consideration.

First, it seems quite appropriate, as well as feasible, to consider that utilization can be manifested in three classical psychological dimensions—behavior, cognition, and emotion. Clear instances of behavioral utilization, that is, changes in individual clinician behavior, have occurred in our study, although the appropriate methodology for using these examples to derive a reliable, quantitative, and comparative index of utilization across service units remains an unsolved problem for us. An attempt to scale utilization by means of self-ratings on a Likert-type scale is now being made in our subsequent study replications.

Second, the cognitive dimension, whether it is called "conceptual" utilization, change in perception of a problem, or increased understanding of an issue, is important in understanding the utilization of evaluation findings. While we have not yet shown definite pre-post changes in cognition due to evaluative feedback, we believe our method of extracting "themes" related to an issue and having these rated by potential utilizers is a substantial improvement over asking someone if his/her thinking has changed as a result of the feedback.

Third, we believe that the emotional or affective impact of utilization has been almost totally overlooked by researchers to date. Yet we are not emotionless machines; and how much one can affect the degree of *caring* or *concern* about an issue may very well be the primary determinant of future changes in behavior or practice. In addition, the strength and nature of preexisting feelings about an issue may be expected to strongly influence the potential utilizers' interest in working with the evaluator and considering the information that the evaluator offers. Results from our simple affective rating scales may help stimulate other researchers to include such measures in their studies of utilization and "impact" of information.

Obviously, what we have presented here generates as many questions as answers to a person seeking to understand and assess the consequences of information feedback. But this may suggest that assessing utilization is a process of refining methodology rather than a fixed set of instruments and techniques. We would recommend that investigators attend as much to development of methodological improvements and innovations in measuring utilization as to the theoretical and substantive issues about knowledge utilization. We feel that the "state of the art" is not mature and that more exchange of ideas and innovative application of new techniques are essential if we are ever to answer the questions of whether, when, and how evaluation feedback is actually utilized.

REFERENCES

FERGUS, E. (1979) Personal communication.
LARSEN, J. K. (1979) "The nature and extent of information utilization." Presented at the annual meeting of Network of Consultants on Knowledge Transfer, Denver, Colorado, March 21-24.
PATTON, M. Q. (1978) "Utilization in practice: An empirical perspective," in M. Q. Patton, Utilization-Focused Evaluation. Beverly Hills, CA: Sage.
RICH, R. F. (1978) "The use of science in policy making: A comparative prospective on science policy," in D. Ashford (ed.) Comparing Public Policies. Beverly Hills, CA: Sage.

6

MEASURING UTILIZATION OF NURSING RESEARCH

Donald C. Pelz

*Center for Research on Utilization
of Scientific Knowledge
University of Michigan*

Jo Anne Horsley

*School of Nursing
University of Michigan*

This article will discuss some results from the CURN project (Conduct and Utilization of Research in Nursing)—a five-year research development project funded by the Department of Health, Education and Welfare's Division of Nursing and carried out under the auspices of the Michigan Nurses Association (Horsley et al., 1978). The general aim of the project was to increase the utilization of research findings in the daily practice of registered nurses. This aim was pursued through two programs: (1) a Research Utilization Program to disseminate current research findings and facilitate organizational modifications required for sound implementation and (2) a Collaborative Research Program to encourage the conduct of collaborative research which is readily transferable to nursing practice. The present article deals only with the first program.

THE RESEARCH UTILIZATION CONTEXT

In Chapter 1 of this volume, Weiss raises several conceptual issues in measuring the utilization of research and evaluation. Some of these issues form a context for the present study and will be addressed before our findings are presented.

What Knowledge Was Being Used?

In the CURN project, three separate kinds of knowledge were being used. Two were major inputs: (1) research findings from scientifically conducted studies on clinical nursing practices and (2) knowledge about how to utilize such findings to modify nursing practice—that is, how to conduct the innovating process as such. A third kind of knowledge was subordinate: (3) evaluations by nursing department staff of specific innovations within the department. In contrast to some other projects reported in this volume, the first two types were not derived from evaluations of agency performance but were generated externally.

Scientific findings on clinical nursing practice. In searching the research literature for scientifically validated innovations in nursing practice, the project followed the guideline that *no single research study is sufficient to justify a new nursing practice.* Replication must occur before the new knowledge is disseminated. Accordingly, the CURN staff generated a set of research-based innovation protocols (3 at the beginning, 10 at present), each based on a series of replicated studies having both scientific and clinical merit. The procedures and criteria used in generating these protocols are described by Haller et al. (1979). The protocols themselves are in the process of being published in 10 volumes (Horsley et al., forthcoming) and comprise: Structured Preoperative Teaching, Decubitus Prevention in Patients at Risk, Reducing Diarrhea in Tube Fed Patients, Deliberative Nursing for Complaint of Pain, Mutual Goal Setting, Closed Urinary Drainage System, Clean Intermittent Self-Catheterization, Intravenous Catheter Change, Distress Reduction through Sensation Information, and Providing Sensation Information to Promote Recovery Rate.

The innovation protocol is the vehicle by which the research knowledge is transformed into clinically useful knowledge and disseminated to service agencies. Each protocol has several components: a statement of the clinical problems which this innovation may address, a summary of the research base, an empirical principle generated from the base, a description of the innovation in terms of practice activity, considerations for implementation, considerations for clinical evaluation, instruments for evaluation, annotated bibliography, and original research reports.

Knowledge about the process of research utilization. Knowledge of the second type was drawn from a wide literature on the innovating process, particularly Havelock's (1969) formulation of a "linkage model" of knowledge use. A major concern was to minimize the risk of misutilization, which might arise from two potential sources. One could occur if invalid knowledge were used as the basis for an innovation; to guard against this source, the innovation protocols were painstakingly developed. A second potential source could arise if valid knowledge were misunderstood and an innovation did not accurately reflect what was known.

Accordingly, a comprehensive process of research utilization (RU) was designed, under the guideline that *knowledge generated in a controlled, scientific context may not be valid when used in an uncontrolled, clinical context.* The process included a detailed training program as summarized in the following section on the CURN intervention. To make proper use of the protocols, and to minimize the risk of misutilization, the training program assisted each experimental site in learning how to identify needs, to select an innovation appropriate to those needs, and to implement and evaluate the innovation so as to make an informed decision on retaining or dropping it. (An account of this RU process will form the eleventh volume in the series by Horsley et al., forthcoming. The rationale of this process is summarized by Crane and Horsley, forthcoming.)

Evaluation of a specific innovation by the department's own staff. To assure that effects of a particular innovation in an uncontrolled, clinical context were reasonably equivalent to those in the controlled, scientific context of the research base, the CURN procedure specified that a local evaluation be done, including both process and outcomes measures, and that at least one of the outcome variables should have been studied in the original research. The protocol for each innovation included potential evaluation instruments, capable of being applied by professionally (but not scientifically) trained nursing staff.

Because of the many sources of noncorrespondence between the scientific context of the research base and the clinical context of its practical application, evaluation of the latter was considered essential for the RU process. Training staff nurses in evaluation methods was one of the most difficult facets of the process, but one of those most valued by participants.

How Direct Was the Derivation of the Knowledge Used?

Two of the above knowledge types were directly derived from their respective sources. Each innovation protocol (type 1) provided a detailed summary of the research findings, specified the patient populations that were and were not appropriate, and considered limitations in translating the research results into practice. In addition, members of the innovation team read the original studies. Data from the local evaluations (type 3) were directly incorporated in reports to nursing decision makers.

Knowledge about the research utilization process (type 2) was derived less directly from original sources. What was used were not findings but principles, based on the guidelines cited above to minimize the risk of misutilization and assure adherence to the research base of type 1.

What Kind of Research Utilization Occurred?

Weiss suggests a continuum ranging from an "instrumental" end where research directly influences decisions to an "understanding" end where research contributes diffusely to an understanding of issues, causes, and intervention dynamics. In the CURN project, much of the knowledge use was of instrumental character. Thus, knowledge about specific innovations (1) was directly incorporated into changes by the department in its ongoing practices. Findings from the department's evaluation of its own innovation (3) were used directly in a decision to continue, expand, or drop the innovation.

Utilization of knowledge about the RU process (2) lay farther toward the "understanding" end of the Weiss continuum. Aside from an initial decision by the nursing director to participate or not, there were no distinct points at which such knowledge affected departmental practices. Rather, over a period of many months, it affected the department's understanding and conduct of the innovating process. Some of these effects, of course, were more direct than others. The most direct effect was conduct of the RU activity itself. Thirteen experimental sites carried out the utilization process. Eleven of these sites were able to demonstrate the predicted results following the innovation trial and evaluation. One site stopped its trial when its baseline evaluation data showed that it did not have the problem it was attempting to solve. In the remaining site, outcome data did not produce a demonstrable patient change following the trial.

Other possible effects could appear in questionnaire data. Relatively direct effects might be a heightened sense—among those nurses involved in the innovating process—that they could review research, could screen and select practice innovation, and could implement and evaluate these. Less direct effects might include subtle changes in attitudes about research and about innovations in practice. Participants might feel greater ability to evaluate their own practice, change it on the basis of new ideas from research, and influence others to make research-based changes. One might expect participants to feel that certain nursing committees had greater influence on the content of nursing practice. In addition, one might expect nursing staff *not* directly involved in the innovating process—such as other supervisory or administrative personnel—to experience some of the same changes.

The third and fourth sections of this article will examine quantitative evidence on occurrence of both direct and indirect effects in the questionnaire data.

Methods for the Study of Use

Later in her chapter Weiss sketches several approaches to study the consequences of research use. The principal method used in the present chapter is that of a *survey questionnaire* answered by staff members of participating hospitals over two yearly intervals. This methodology will be described in our third section.

In addition, CURN staff kept detailed records using the strategy of *participant observation.* These observations formed the basis for qualitative judgments of three dimensions: (1) supportiveness of the hospital environment toward the RU concept; (2) learning of RU process by the innovation team; and (3) innovation team outcomes—adequacy and quality. The ratings were performed independently by two CURN staff members each responsible for two series of RU workshops. (These judgments were made only on experimental hospitals, of course, not on comparative ones.)

Under the first dimension of supportiveness, the two judges rated each of five components on 7-point scales: director of nursing supportive; upper-level staff sympathetic; staff nurses cooperative; ongoing operations of department or hospital free from major disruptions; absence of staff shortages. Under the second dimension of process learning, five components were rated: innovation team receptive to RU concept; team coordinator effective and continuing; team members work well together without internal conflict; team members understand RU process; team applies RU process effectively. Under the third dimension of outcomes, four components were rated: effective materials and coaching of people to implement the process; process carried through to completion; outcomes of high merit or quality; team activities approximate methodology; and content of research base.

For each judge, scores on the several components were summed to obtain an index on each dimension, and Spearman rank-order correlations were computed between the indexes of the two judges on each dimension. For the first two workshop series, the two training directors had kept in close touch with each other's workshops. For these six hospitals, the interjudge rank-order correlations for the three dimensions were respectively: .99, .63, and .94. The directors had less contact across the next two workshop series for the last seven hospitals (in fact, only five of these hospitals were rated by both judges on dimensions 2 and 3). For the total set of 11 to 13 hospitals, therefore, rank-order correlations for the three dimensions tended to drop: .94, .73, and .63, respectively.

In sum, these data indicate that interjudge reliability was high for the judgment of supportiveness of hospital environment and moderate on judgments of RU process and outcomes. Participant observation offers promise for measuring utilization of nursing research. But for the present article, we have not examined relationships of these judgments to the survey data.

THE CURN INTERVENTION: RESEARCH UTILIZATION PROCESS

As mentioned above, a research utilization training program was developed following two major guidelines, to assist each nursing department in conducting an innovating process. The training program was carried out in four series of seven workshops which took nine full working days over a nine-month period.

To carry out this process, each department of nursing appointed an Innovation Team (IT) of six to eight staff members who participated in the training program and bore responsibility for actually implementing one of the research-based innovation protocols as they proceeded through training. Attending each seminar were ITs from two to four hospitals, grouped either by geographical area or by interinstitutional merger agreements. This format increased the opportunity to form long-term supportive relationships among the teams.

Innovation Team members were selected jointly by the director of nursing and the CURN Project staff member responsible for a workshop series. Members were selected so as to assure several characteristics: formal organizational influence, informal influence or opinion leadership, clinical expertise, and representation of the nursing staff population (i.e., by shift, position, and ethnicity). A coordinator was chosen who would provide leadership, would know the organization, would dedicate time and effort, and especially would have the nursing director's confidence. A typical Innovation Team might include these roles: Associate Director of Nursing (team coordinator), Supervisory (evenings), Head Nurse (medical), Head Nurse (surgical), Staff Nurse (nights), Staff Development Director, Quality Assurance Coordinator. Innovation Team roles thus resembled the administrative and supervisory roles in the department (aside from one or two Staff Nurses).

Each workshop took up one or two phases of a knowledge-based innovating process and gave assignments on that topic to be carried out in the following weeks, with experiences to be reported at the next seminar. The workshops in succession dealt with such topics as: general concepts of research utilization process; how to identify patient problems for which research-based solutions were available; how to select an appropriate innovation which both met a high-priority need and had good adoption potential; planning the change that would be implemented in one pilot unit; handling the inevitable problems during actual implementation; dealing with resistance to change; evaluating the trial implementation; interpreting such data for use in a decision to retain or discontinue the innovation; planning for extension of the innovation (if retained) to other nursing units in the hospital.

Principles of the research utilization process were repeatedly used in every step of this training program. Although each topic was addressed in specific workshops, most of them were repeatedly readdressed throughout the series.

A three-month interval elapsed between seminars six or seven, during which the IT carried out the trial and evaluated it, maintaining contact with project staff by telephone or occasional visits.

As indicated earlier, 13 of the 15 experimental hospitals carried out this RU project to its completion, and 11 of the sites were able to demonstrate the predicted results following trial and evaluation.

MEASUREMENT OF CHANGE USING SURVEY DATA

Population and Research Design

The CURN research utilization program was undertaken in a stratified probability sample of Michigan hospitals which had at least 100 beds (excluding long-term or psychiatric facilities), met standards of the Joint Committee on Accreditation of Hospitals, and were situated in the southern half of the state where two-thirds of the hospital beds are located. Hospitals were first assigned to clusters based on geographic proximity or interinstitutional merger agreements. Under stratification by size of hospitals in the cluster and location (Detroit metropolitan area versus other areas), clusters were randomly assigned to experimental and comparison groups.

The research utilization program was introduced in nursing departments of the 17 hospitals comprising the experimental group. Two of these hospitals were used as pilot sites (data not reported here) and two dropped out during the first year. The remaining 13 received the full training program described above.

Questionnaires were administered in the 17 experimental hospitals and in 15 comparison hospitals at three periods: before the intervention, one year later, and in half the sites two years later.

Within each participating hospital, survey respondents were drawn from selected medical/surgical nursing units. Unit selection was decided on the basis of where the project's research-based practice innovations were most likely to be implemented. There was an average of 50 respondents in each participating hospital. Respondents in each site varied from year to year, of course, because of self-selection and turnover. In each hospital site, all of the registered nurses who worked on or directly influenced the quality of patient care on the selected units were invited to participate, plus all supervisory, administrative, and staff development personnel linked with these units. Of those invited to participate, 69% did so; response rate per site varied from 58% to 81%.

Within each experimental hospital, at each time period, we shall examine questionnaire data from two groups: (1) all members of the department's ITs and (2) all *other* staff members in four upper-level roles—hereafter called the non-ITs: Administrator (director of nursing and associate/ assistant directors), Supervisor, Staff Development personnel, and Head Nurse. We shall not examine data for the bulk of personnel in Staff Nurse roles, or for a few in Clinical Specialist or "other" roles. It was felt that most Staff Nurses (aside from a few serving on an IT) had little involvement in the innovation process, although they would of course carry out the selected innovation in trial units. Furthermore, a previous analysis revealed that RU scores of this group showed almost no differentiation across hospitals.[1]

In each experimental hospital, data were obtained from about 6 IT members (the range per hospital was 2-9) and from about 9 non-IT members in the four upper roles (the range per hospital was 4-32). We did not exclude the few Staff Nurses serving on ITs. Otherwise the role membership of the IT and non-IT groups was comparable. Our analysis procedure was not affected by the size of these groups, since (as explained below) we used mean scores of each IT and non-IT group within each hospital. For significance testing, what mattered was the number of hospitals.

For testing differences between experimental and comparison hospitals, it was necessary to form an "artificial Innovation Team" within each of the latter. The typical role membership of an IT was described earlier. In each comparison hospital, seven comparable roles were designated, and one person in each of these roles was randomly selected to comprise the "artificial IT" group for that hospital. The remaining persons in upper-level roles for that hospital constituted its "non-IT" group.

Instruments

The data were generated by an 18-page machine-scored questionnaire, administered in each participating site at selected 2 to 3-hour intervals on each work shift. Potential respondents were contacted by a personal letter three to four days in advance, which described aims and procedures, and were assured of their department's approval of the study and confidentiality of responses. At the time of administration, a project data collector notified the units that she was available in the designated room, where respondents filled out the questionnaire. Data collection was repeated until 70% of potential respondents had participated, or until five collection days were completed. These procedures were applied in 1977, but modified in the next two years because of severe staffing shortages in the hospitals.

From some 430 items of information obtained from the questionnaires, 10 items and one index were selected as measuring, directly or indirectly, the extent of RU.

Direct measures. Five items under Question 19 described explicit RU activities: "We are interested in knowing how often you have engaged in the following research activities during the past year," with a response scale of 0, 1, 2-4, 5 or more times in past year:

(1) You reviewed research literature in an effort to identify new knowledge for use in your practice.
(2) You evaluated a research study to determine its value for practice.
(3) You transferred the knowledge included in the results of the research studies into useful practice activities.
(4) You planned for the implementation and evaluation of new research-based practices.
(5) You discontinued or rejected a practice activity because of knowledge included in the results of research studies.

Under a process of index construction for the whole questionnaire, we had formed clusters of items that were at least moderately intercorrelated within each of the five role categories. The above five items met the criterion and were combined into an RU index for each respondent, derived from the mean frequency of the components. (Another item under Question 19, "You attended research conferences and heard about new studies," did not meet the criterion and was excluded.) The Cronbach alpha of this index, for all non-Staff Nurses in year 1 in both intervention and comparison hospitals, was .87.

Indirect measures. Five other items also appeared to measure research utilization less directly. Question 11 asked the extent to which several possible types of committees "influence nursing practice in your hospital" (on a 5-point scale from None to Complete), where nursing practice included "direct care activities and the formulation of policies which govern direct care activities." Two such committees were defined as responsible for:

(1) identifying, selecting, and implementing *new nursing* practices
(2) evaluating effectiveness of *current and new nursing* practices.

Such committees might or might not exist at a given site. If they did not (which was generally the case), their influence would be rated low, or the rating omitted. After an IT was formed, it should take on precisely the functions listed above. If the team were effective, one would expect the above ratings to rise, among both IT and non-IT staff.

At another point, Question 35 asked to what extent (on a 5-point scale from No extent to Very great) the respondent can do a series of activities in her own job, including:

(1) evaluate your practice
(2) alter your own nursing practice based on new ideas
(3) influence others to alter their nursing practice based on new ideas.

If the intervention were having its intended effect, one might expect a larger rise on these items for IT members than for non-IT staff.

Hypotheses

The survey data were analyzed to test several expectations.

1. Before intervention, one would expect to find no difference in reported research utilization between (1) ITs and the non-ITs (upper four roles) in the experimental hospitals nor between (2) ITs in experimental hospitals and the "artificial ITs" in comparison hospitals.

2. Over the first-year interval of the intervention, and continuing for a second year in half the hospitals, one would expect IT members to gain substantially in RU scores, whereas non-IT members would gain a smaller amount, if any.

3. Accordingly, in year 2 and continuing in year 3, IT members in experimental hospitals should measure substantially higher in RU scores than (1) their non-IT counterparts in the same hospitals and higher than (2) the artificial ITs in comparison hospitals.

4. However, if skill or interest in research utilization diffused as intended from IT members to other staff in the same hospitals, we should observe (1) slight increases over time among non-ITs in experimental hospitals and a drop in the differences between the two groups but (2) no changes over time in the comparison hospital, either in the artificial ITs or the non-ITs.

RESULTS

To test the hypothesized differences between ITs and non-ITs in the same hospital (as in Table 1A), we obtained the mean on each measure for the IT group and the non-IT group, respectively, and applied a method of paired t tests between the two sets of group means.[2] This method recognizes and partials out the fact that IT and non-IT members in the same hospital may be similar. The method also increases precision by removing individual variance within each group.

To test the hypothesized changes in either ITs or non-ITs over time (as in Tables 2 and 3), a similar method of paired t test was applied, based on differences in group means in the same hospital (for ITs or non-ITs, respectively) between successive years. Because of the pairing, only hospitals having data in both years could be used.

To test differences between ITs in experimental hospitals and the artificial ITs in comparison hospitals (as in Table 1B), we again used group means in each hospital, but these could not be paired. A simple t test was done between the two sets of group means.

Hypothesis 1

Before intervention, one would expect to find no differences between ITs and non-ITs in experimental hospitals nor between ITs in experimental sites and "artificial ITs" in comparison sites. The corresponding results are given for *year 1* in Tables 1A and 1B, respectively.

In year 1 there were no significant differences between experimental IT members and non-IT staff on any of the five direct research utilization activities or the RU index (top of Table 1A). Apparently, IT members were not selected because they were more proinnovation than their peers. If anything, they were slightly less so than the remaining upper-level staff (one of these negative differences was of borderline significance, $p < .10$).

For the indirect measures also (bottom of Table 1A), experimental IT members at year 1 were not more proinnovation than their non-IT peers; on the last measure, in fact, they were significantly less so.

Likewise at year 1, IT groups in experimental hospitals tended to be slightly less innovative than the artificial ITs in comparison sites (Table 1B).

Hypothesis 2

Over the one- or two-year span of the intervention, one would expect experimental IT groups to gain substantially in direct RU scores, and

(text continued on page 140)

TABLE 1: Difference on Research Utilization Measures Using Group Means, between (A) Experimental IT and Non-IT Mean of Means, and (B) Experimental ITs and Comparison ITs (Artificial)[a]

DIRECT MEASURES (Q 19)[e]	Year[b]	A. Experimental			B. Comparative	
		ITs	ITs	Difference[c] IT – N-IT	ITs	Difference[d] Exp.-Comp.
Reviewed research lit. to identify new knowledge for use in practice	1	2.37	2.59	– .22	2.82	– .45+
	2	3.69	2.61	1.08**	2.81	.88*
	3	3.23	2.63	.60	2.50	.73
Evaluated research study to determine value for practice	1	1.33	1.29	.04	1.48	– .15
	2	3.25	1.55	1.70**	1.19	2.06**
	3	2.49	1.69	.80+	1.02	1.47*
Transferred knowledge into useful practice activities	1	1.01	1.23	– .22	1.38	– .37+
	2	2.64	1.23	1.41**	1.27	1.37**
	3	1.68	1.34	.34	.90	.78
Discontinued practice activity because of research knowledge	1	.55	.62	– .07	.67	– .12
	2	1.11	.51	.60*	.57	.54*
	3	1.12	.77	.35	.35	.77*
Research utilization index: mean of above 5 items	1	1.20	1.36	– .16	1.45	– .25
	2	2.69	1.37	1.32**	1.34	1.35**
	3	2.06	1.55	.51+	1.02	1.04**

TABLE 1 continued

DIRECT MEASURES (Q 19)[e]	Year[b]	A. Experimental		Difference[c] IT – N-IT	B. Comparative	Difference[d] Exp.-Comp.
		ITs	ITs		ITs	
INDIRECT MEASURES						
Influence[f] on nursing pract. by committees for (Q 11):						
–Identifying and implementing new nursing practices	1	3.61	3.44	.17	3.47	.14
	2	3.57	3.53	.04	3.67	-.10
	3	3.91	3.82	.09	3.09	.82+
Evaluating effectiveness of practices (current and new)	1	3.53	3.44	.09	3.44	.09
	2	3.64	3.45	.19	3.69	-.05
	3	3.89	3.76	.13	3.24	.65
To what extent[g] Respondent can (Q 35):						
–Evaluate own practice	1	3.82	3.78	.04	3.72	.10
	2	3.76	3.75	.01	3.68	.08
	3	4.13	4.05	.08	4.07	.06
–Alter own practice based on new ideas	1	3.53	3.69	-.16	3.60	-.07
	2	3.52	3.65	-.13	3.65	-.13
	3	3.61	3.82	-.21	3.81	-.20

TABLE 1 continued

DIRECT MEASURES (Q 19)[e]	Year[b]	A. Experimental		Difference[c] IT – N-IT	B. Comparative		Difference[d] Exp.-Comp.
		ITs	ITs		ITs		
—Influence others to	1	3.36	3.65	-.29*		3.44	-.08
alter practice based	2	3.41	3.66	-.25		3.54	-.13
on new ideas	3	3.67	3.80	-.13		3.69	-.02

[a]See text for full description of measures.
[b]Hospital Ns were:

	Exper.	Compar.
Year1	15	15
Year 2	13	15
Year 3	6	9

[c]Significance of difference was tested by simple t-test between hospital means, where: + = $p<.10$; * = $p<.05$; ** = $p<.01$.
[d]Significance of difference was tested by simple t-test between sets of means for Experimental and Comparison sites. Same symbols as above.
[e]Number of times Respondent has done this in past year.
[f]On 5-point scale where 1 = None, 3 = Moderate, 5 = Complete.
[g]On 5-point scale where 1 = No extent, 3 = Some, 5 = Very great extent.

139

perhaps slightly in the indirect scores, but non-IT groups should gain little if any. Data for IT members are presented in Table 2 and for non-ITs in Table 3. Because only hospitals with data in both years could be used, the means will differ slightly from those in Table 1.

Direct measures. For each of the six RU activity scores (top of Table 2), the experimental IT members increased significantly from year 1 to year 2 (mostly $p < .01$). These gains tended to shrink in year 3, so that the differences over the two-year span were smaller, and only four of the six were significant ($p < .05$, based on six hospitals only).

The right-hand column of Table 2 illustrates the shrinkage during the second year. Five of the six RU scores dropped slightly, but only one of them significantly so.

In short, *effects of the intervention on IT members persisted over the second year,* but less sharply than was evident over the first year.

The top of Table 3 displays comparable data for experimental non-IT staff. There were no significant changes over any of three time intervals. However, note that over the two-year span, and also during the second year, four of the five items plus the RU index showed consistent slight gains. Conceivably, the sharp gains experienced by IT members between years 1 and 2 may have seeped into the thinking of their upper-level colleagues and modified the climate, producing a *mildly positive change by year 3.*

If such slight changes were genuine, one can ask whether they resulted from the project intervention or were part of a general trend in Michigan hospitals. That question can be answered by examining data for comparison hospitals over the same interval—see results under hypothesis 4.

Indirect measures. For the other five items (bottom of Tables 2 and 3), results were ambiguous.

If the ITs began to influence nursing practice in their respective hospitals, scores on Question 11 concerning two committees should rise both for ITs themselves and for non-IT members. In Table 2, however, IT members showed no significant changes over any of the three time intervals. Either the IT members did not recognize their committee in these descriptions or they did not believe that the influence of their committee had risen.

In Question 35 about their own jobs, respondents rated their ability to do several things in their current position. If the intervention changed how IT members performed their own jobs, they ought to feel more able to evaluate their own practice, to alter their own practice based on new ideas,

(text continued on page 145)

TABLE 2: Changes on Research Utilization Variables over Three Years: Experimental Group Means for IT Members[a]

DIRECT MEASURES (Q 19)	N[b]	Mean of Means			Difference in Means[c]		
		Year 1	Year 2	Year 3	Y2-Y1	Y3-Y1	Y3-Y2
Reviewed research lit. to ident. new knowl.	13	2.36	3.69	3.23	1.33**		
	6	2.19	3.36			1.04*	-.13
Eval. research study to det. practice value	13	1.28	3.25	2.49	1.97**		
	6	.99	3.04			1.50*	-.55
Transferred knowl. into useful pract. activ.	13	1.12	2.65	1.68	1.53**		
	6	1.12	2.58			.56	.90+
Planned implement./eval. of new practices	13	.75	2.73	1.74	1.98**		
	6	.80	2.85			.94**	-1.11*
Discontin'd pract. activ. because of res. knowl.	13	.58	1.11	1.12	.53*		
	6	.51	1.21			.61+	-.09
Research utiliz. index: mean of above 5 items	13	1.23	2.69	2.06	1.46**		
	6	1.15	2.60			.91**	-.54

141

TABLE 2 continued

	N^b						
INDIRECT MEASURES							
Influence by committees for (Q 11):							
—Ident./implementing new practices	13	3.78	3.57		-.21		.15
	6	3.99	3.76	3.91		-.08	
—Evaluating effectiveness of practices	13	3.62	3.64		.02		.04
	6	3.77	3.85	3.89		.12	
To what extent can Respondent (Q 35):							
—Evaluate own practice	13	3.87	3.76		-.11		.31
	6	3.87	3.82	4.13		.26*	
—Alter own practice based on new ideas	13	3.56	3.52		-.04		.09
	6	3.56	3.52	3.61		.05	
—Infl. others to alter ...based on new ideas	13	3.42	3.41		-.01		.20
	6	3.49	3.47	3.67		.18	

[a]Same footnotes apply as in Table 1

[b]Number of hospitals will vary since cross-year comparisons use only hospitals with data in both years.

[c]Significance of difference was tested by paired t-test between group means, where: + = p<.10; * = p<.05; ** = p<.01.

TABLE 3: Changes on Research Utilization Variables over Three Years: Experimental Group Means for Non-IT Staff[a]

DIRECT MEASURES (Q 19)	N	Mean of Means			Difference in Means[b]		
		Year 1	Year 2	Year 3	Y2-Y1	Y3-Y1	Y3-Y2
Reviewed research lit. to ident. new knowl.	13	2.52	2.61	2.63	.09	.02	.01
	6	2.61	2.62				
Eval. research study to det. practice value	13	1.22	1.55	1.69	.33	.48	.24
	6	1.21	1.45				
Transferred knowl. into useful pract. activ.	13	1.18	1.23	1.34	.05	.15	.30
	6	1.19	1.04				
Planned implement./eval. of new practices	13	.99	.88	1.34	-.11	.49	.54
	6	.85	.80				
Discontin'd pract. activ. because of res. knowl.	13	.56	.51	.77	-.05	.11	.42
	6	.66	.35				
Research utiliz. index: mean of above 5 items	13	1.31	1.37	1.55	.06	.21	.28
	6	1.34	1.27				

TABLE 3 continued

INDIRECT MEASURES

	N					
Influence by committees for (Q11):						
—Ident./implementing new practices	13	3.52	3.53	.01		
	6	3.51	3.49		.31+	.33
—Evaluating effectiveness of practices	13	3.51	3.45		.17	
	6	3.58	3.62	-.06		.13+
To what extent can Respondent (Q35):						
—Evaluate own practice	13	3.80	3.75	-.05		
	6	3.90	3.83		.15	.21
—Alter own practice based on new ideas	13	3.67	3.65	-.02		
	6	3.69	3.66		.13	.16
—Infl. others to alter . . .based on new ideas	13	3.64	3.66	.02		
	6	3.67	3.73		.13	.07

[a]Same footnotes apply as in Tables 1 and 2.

[b]Significance tested by paired t-test between departmental means, where: + = $p < .10$.

144

and to influence others to do so. As shown in the bottom of Table 2, IT members showed no change on these items during the first year, but mildly positive gains thereafter (one of these was significant, $p < .05$).

Table 3 shows data for non-IT staff over comparable intervals. Like the IT data, no changes at all appeared during the first year. But during the second year, and over the two-year span, *all five measures showed mild gains* (two of them were of borderline significance).

In short, there was a slight hint of delayed effects in the indirect measure. In subtle ways the intervention may have raised the RU climate during the second year.

Hypothesis 3

As a result of the above changes over time, IT members in experimental hospitals should measure higher at years 2 and 3 than their non-IT peers in the same hospitals (Table 1A) and higher than the artificial ITs in comparison hospitals (Table 1B).

Direct measures. One year after the project started (year 2), experimental ITs were significantly higher than their non-IT counterparts on all six RU measures (top of Table 1A). They were also significantly higher than the artificial ITs in comparison hospitals, on all of the RU scores (top of Table 1B).

Data for two years later (year 3) were available for only half the hospitals. In these, the experimental ITs continued to score higher than non-ITs on all six measures, but the differences were smaller and nonsignificant (top of Table 1A). This diminished difference arose mainly from a drop in the IT scores but also from a slight rise in non-IT scores.

In year 3, however, experimental ITs continued to score significantly above the comparison ITs on four of the six RU scores (top of Table 1B). This trend resulted from the sharp drop in comparison scores.

Indirect measures. One year after the project began (year 2), there were no significant differences between experimental ITs and their counterpart non-ITs on any of these five scores (bottom of Table 1A). Nor were there any significant differences after two years (year 3). A close look at these data, however, will reveal that the scores for *both* ITs and non-ITs tended to creep upward from year 1 to 3.

When experimental ITs were tested against comparison ITs (bottom of Table 2B), no clear trends appeared.

Hypothesis 4

If interest in RU has diffused from IT members to other upper-level staff in the same hospital, we should observe slight increases over time among *experimental non-ITs* but not among *comparison* non-ITs.

The picture for experimental non-ITs is shown in Table 3. Over the first year (see column headed Y2-Y1), differences were very slight, and equally positive and negative. Over the second year (column headed Y3-Y2), however, and over the two-year span (column headed Y3-Y1), all differences were positive.

Data for comparison non-ITs are given in Table 4. There were no significant (or even borderline) differences between experimental and comparison non-ITs in any of the three years, although over time the differences tended to favor the experimental groups on some items.

SUMMARY

One aim of the CURN project was to help hospital nursing departments to apply scientific findings on clinical nursing in the daily practice of registered nurses. To guard against misutilization, either from use of invalid knowledge or from misunderstanding of valid knowledge as the basis for an innovation, the project staff generated 10 innovation protocols based on replicated studies having both scientific and clinical merit, and trained an Innovation Team from each hospital in a research utilization process through a series of seven workshops over a nine-month period. This process included an evaluation by the department's staff of its own innovation.

In terms of Weiss's continuum on type of utilization (in her Chapter 1 here), the innovation protocols and the evaluation results were utilized near the "instrumental" end of this continuum, as evidenced by the fact that 13 of 15 experimental sites completed the program, and 11 of these were able to demonstrate the predicted results following innovation trial and evaluation. Utilization of principles of RU in the training program occurred farther toward the "understanding" end of the Weiss continuum.

Evidence on the latter use was examined in questionnaire responses from stratified probability samples of experimental and comparison hospitals, on which three waves of survey data had been obtained at annual intervals.

TABLE 4: Differences on Research Utilization Measures between Experimental and Comparison Non-ITs, Using Group Means[a]

| | | Mean of Means | | |
	Year[b]	Exper. Non-ITs	Compar. Non-ITs	Difference:[c] Exp.-Comp.
DIRECT MEASURES (Q 19)				
Reviewed research lit. to	1	2.64	2.48	.16
identify new knowledge	2	2.70	2.53	.17
	3	2.66	2.54	.12
Evaluated research study	1	1.22	1.19	.03
to determine practice	2	1.55	1.34	.21
value	3	1.71	1.01	.70
Transferred knowledge	1	1.16	1.16	.00
into useful practice	2	1.19	1.14	.05
activity	3	1.36	.92	.44
Planned implementation	1	.94	.93	.01
and evaluation of new	2	.89	.83	.06
practices	3	1.34	.73	.61
Discontinued practice	1	.58	.52	.06
activity becasue of	2	.52	.46	.06
research knowledge	3	.78	.55	.23
Research utilization	1	1.32	1.29	.03
index: mean of	2	1.38	1.26	.12
above 5 items	3	1.56	1.15	.41
INDIRECT MEASURES				
Influence by committees for (Q 11):				
–Identifying and	1	3.43	3.54	- .11
implementing new	2	3.55	3.46	.09
practices	3	3.82	3.52	.30
–Evaluating effective-	1	3.49	3.43	.06
ness of practice	2	3.46	3.31	.15
	3	3.76	3.51	.25
To what extent Respondent can (Q 35):				
–Evaluate own practice	1	3.75	3.86	- .11
	2	3.74	3.81	- .07
	3	4.07	3.77	.30
–Alter own practice	1	3.65	3.77	- .12
based on new ideas	2	3.66	3.70	- .04
	3	3.85	3.84	.01

147

TABLE 4 continued

| | Year[b] | Mean of Means | | Difference:[c] Exp.-Comp. |
		Exper. Non-ITs	Compar. Non-ITs	
−Influence others to	1	3.64	3.72	- .08
alter practice based	2	3.66	3.68	- .02
on new ideas	3	3.81	3.77	.04

[a]Same footnotes apply as in previous tables.

[b]Hospital Ns were:

	Exper.	Compar.
Year 1	15	15
Year 2	13	15
Year 3	6	9

[c]Significance tested by simple t-test between sets of group means for Experimental and Comparison sites. None of the differences had a $p < .10$.

"Direct" measures of RU were five items and a summary index about reviewing and evaluating research studies and implementing and evaluating research-based practices. Indirect measures included perception of how certain committees influenced nursing practice, and the respondent's felt ability to alter and evaluate her own practice based on new ideas, and influence others to do likewise. Data were examined from ITs and from non-ITs and from comparison hospitals in which "artificial ITs" were formed by random selection of staff members in comparable roles.

Over the first year in which the training occurred, ITs in experimental hospitals gained significantly in the direct measures; at the end of this year they scored significantly higher than two similar groups—non-ITs in the same hospitals and artificial ITs in comparison hospitals. Although these gains tended to shrink over the next year, effects of the intervention in the direct measures persisted over two years. Indirect measures, for the most part, showed no significant changes.

For non-IT staff, no changes at all appeared during the first year, but over the two-year span there were consistent slight gains in both direct and indirect measures. Hence there was some hint that the sharp initial gains by IT members may have seeped into the thinking of their colleagues and raised the research utilization climate during the second year—a utilization effect toward the "understanding" end of the Weiss continuum.

NOTES

1. On the RU index described below, departmental means were obtained separately for Staff Nurses and non-Staff Nurses. For the former, differences among hospitals accounted for only 1.6% of the RU index variance ($p = .84$), whereas for the latter, differences among hospitals accounted for 9.6% of the variance ($p = .16$).

2. See, for example, Lindquist (1940: 58-59). As an illustration: to test the significance of difference between ITs and non-ITs on the RU index in year 1 (as in Table 1A), obtain the difference between the means in each pair in each of 15 hospitals, use the distribution of differences to estimate the standard error, and test the hypothesis that the mean of this distribution = 0.

REFERENCES

CRANE, J. and J. A. HORSLEY (forthcoming) "Introducing change in nursing: Utilization of scientific knowledge in clinical practice," in J. Krueger and R. Luke (eds.) Quality Assurance: Administrative and Organizational Issues. Germantown, MD: Aspen Systems Corporation.

HALLER, K. B., M. A. REYNOLDS, and J. A. HORSLEY (1979) "Developing research-based innovation protocols: Process, criteria, and issues." Research in Nursing and Health 2 (June): 45-51.

HAVELOCK, R. G. (1969) Planning for innovation through dissemination and utilization of knowledge. Ann Arbor: University of Michigan, Center for Research on Utilization of Scientific Knowledge.

HORSLEY, J. A., J. CRANE, and J. D. BINGLE (forthcoming) Using Research To Improve Nursing Practice. New York: Grune & Stratton.

——— (1978) "Research utilization as an organizational process." Journal of Nursing Administration 8(7): 4-6.

LINDQUIST, E. F. (1940) Statistical Analysis in Education Research. Boston: Houghton-Mifflin.

ABOUT THE CONTRIBUTORS

Cathy D. Anderson, Ph.D., is an experimental psychologist and a Research Associate on the staff of the Mental Health Systems Evaluation Project. She received her doctorate from the University of Colorado and is also affiliated with the University of Colorado Health Sciences Center, where she works on psychophysiological research on stress-related disorders.

Susan F. Brodie, M.A., received her degree in sociology from the University of Denver. She was a Research Associate with the Mental Health Systems Evaluation Project when the research reported in her article was conducted.

James A. Ciarlo, Ph.D., is a Research Professor at the University of Denver. He directs the Mental Health Systems Evaluation Project, which is sponsored jointly by the university and the Mental Health Program of Denver's Department of Health and Hospitals. His research involvements include the development of evaluation instruments and techniques, their application to Denver's mental health services, and the use of evaluation feedback in program change. He received his doctorate from Harvard University in clinical psychology and has been coeditor of the *Community Mental Health Journal* since 1978.

Ross F. Conner is Associate Professor in the Program in Social Ecology and Research Psychologist in the Public Policy Research Organization, both at the University of California, Irvine. He received his master's and doctoral degrees in social psychology from Northwestern University. He is the coauthor of *Sesame Street Revisited* and *Attorneys as Activists: Evaluating the American Bar Association's BASICS Program* and the author of a number of articles on evaluation research. His current work focuses on the ethics of using control-group research designs in evaluation projects, participants' reactions to randomization in evaluation research programs, and the evaluation of research utilization. For the 1980-1981 academic year, he is on leave, working in Washington, DC, with the Office of the Director of the Peace Corps on evaluation planning, implementation, and utilization.

Jo Anne Horsley, R.N., Ph.D., F.A.A.N., is Professor of Nursing and acting chairperson of Medical-Surgical Nursing, University of Michigan School of Nursing. She is principal investigator on the CURN project and coauthor of *Using Research To Improve Nursing Practice* (New York: Grune & Stratton, forthcoming).

Judith K. Larsen is a Senior Research Scientist with the American Institutes for Research in Palo Alto, California. Her major research interests are knowledge transfer and utilization. Currently she is directing a study of information utilization in mental health services. She is Executive Editor of *Innovations: Highlights of Evolving Mental Health Services* and R&D Management Practices Editor of *Knowledge: Creation, Diffusion, and Utilization.*

Donald C. Pelz, Ph.D., is a program director in the Center for Research on Utilization of Scientific Knowledge, Institute for Social Research, University of Michigan, and Professor of Psychology. He has been collaborating with staff of the University of Michigan School of Nursing on the five-year CURN Project—Conduct and Utilization of Research in Nursing—to assist nursing departments in Michigan hospitals to develop an innovation process whereby findings from nursing research can be implemented in the daily practice of registered nurses. Other recent activities include the development of a conceptual framework on the innovating process in organizations and a study of innovations in local governments. He has authored (with Frank M. Andrews) *Scientists in Organizations: Productive Climates for Research and Development.*

John F. Stevenson received his Ph.D. in psychology from the University of Michigan. He is Associate Professor of Psychology at the University of Rhode Island. His research interests include evaluation of mental health programs, utilization of evaluation, and learning to cope with organizational stressors.

Carol H. Weiss is a sociologist at the Harvard University Graduate School of Education. She has written extensively about evaluation research, survey research methods, and federal research management. Her earlier work led to a concern with the consequences of social science research for public policy, a subject she has now been studying, writing, consulting, and worrying about for seven years. Her latest books are *Using Social Research for Public Policy Making* and *Social Science Research and Decision-Making.*

Paul D. Werner is Associate Research Scientist at American Institutes for Research in the Behavioral Sciences in Palo Alto, California, and Research Psychologist at the Palo Alto Veterans Administration Medical Center. He received his doctorate in Psychology from the University of California, Berkeley, and has taught at Rutgers University and California School of Professional Psychology. Dr. Werner's interests are in study of personality and social psychological factors in health, mental health, and social change. He has coauthored articles on family planning decision making, activism regarding abortion, assessment of violence in psychiatric patients, and consultation to community mental health centers.